A Critical Analysis of Vijay Tendulkar's

Ghashiram Kotwal

Dr. Beena A. Mahida

CANADIAN

Academic Publishing

2014

Price : $27.86

First Edition : December, 2014

ISBN :   978-1-926488-17-2

ISBN Allotment Agency : Library and Archives Canada (Govt. of Canada)

Published & Printed by
Canadian Academic Publishing
81, Woodlot Crescent,
Etobicoke,
Toronto, Ontario, Canada.
Postal Code- M9W 6T3
Phone- +1 (647) 633 9712
http://www.canadapublish.com

PREFACE

Drama has always remained a unique means to spread morality and to entertain. Long before movies came into being Indian theatre had been a major source of spreading moral value and entertainment. The remarkable feature is that- in spite of the emergence of the Indian cinema, the Indian theatre has not lost significance.

Drama in India has a long history and in regional languages it is as popular as other literary genres – fiction and poetry. In Indian Literature, drama in English has not attained much popularity because plays in regional languages dominate the theatre. In recent times, Plays in the regional languages are translated in to English and such translations have established link between East and West, and North and South as well as harmony and unity in modern India.

In this context Vijay Tendulkar's Marathi Plays occupy a unique place. When I read the English translation of Tendulkar's plays I decided to pursue my research on plays of Tendulkar and in this decision Dr.R.K.Madalia of the Department of English provided much needed help by accepting to become my Supervisor for the research. He suggested to carry out my research on Tendulkar's major 6 (six) plays and to analyse them from the point of view of characterization, themes and dramatic techniques. Each of the plays of Tendulkar presented new perspective which made stimulating reading.

Tendulkar has not contributed to the modern Marathi theatre but has given it a new dimension. His plays disturb the audience by raising complex issues that remain unsettled even today in modern

India. Tendulkar is not feminist but women are at the center in his plays. He treats his women characters with understanding and compassion against men who are selfish and hypocritical.

I have tried my level best in analyzing the different aspects of Tendulkar's Plays yet I believe that literature offers vast spectrum and if something is left out in my research, I leave it to future scholars to pursue studies that are more elaborate. This book is slight modification of the thesis. I have separated each play for a separate book to get wider information regarding the play and the details within and tried to focus in details the themes, characters, and important aspects.

Ghashiram Kotwal is set in eighteenth century Pune at the time of the Peshwa rule. The play features the Peshwa's chancellor Nana Phadnavs and when it was first staged it came up against a lot of criticism of or showing the revered Nana's character in a derogatory light. In my view Ghashiram Kotwal indicates a particular social situation which is neither old nor new. It is beyond time and space. Therefore 'Ghashiram' and Nana Phadnavis are are also beyond space and time'.

The success or failure of any work of art depends upon its appeal – whether that appeal proves to be transitory or everlasting. A work of art with an everlasting appeal always remains eternal. It will not be out of the way or excessive exaggeration if the same thing is said about Tendulkar's plays.

Dr. Beena A. Mahida

CONTENTS

1. INTRODUCTION

In literary criticism, Art is divided into two types. Fine Arts and other than Fine Arts. The function of fine arts is to afford pleasure while other arts satisfy human needs. Architecture, sculpture, music and poetry are fine arts. Drama is included in Fine arts. Other literary forms find expression in statement but drama finds expression in acting. Compared to other literary forms drama is very close to human life hence it is said "Drama makes the spectators hearts dance" Drama is said to be the mirror of the world because on its small scale the full context of human life is revealed. It is a process that originates in the writer's mind and completes itself when it touches the heart of the spectators. It is a world of make-believe and its roots are in performance.

Drama has always remained a unique means to spread morality and to entertain. Long before movies came into being Indian theatre had been a major source of spreading moral value and entertainment. The remarkable feature is that- in spite of the emergence of the Indian cinema, the Indian theatre has not lost significance.

The Indian cinema with all its advanced techniques, sophisticated cameras and freedom of variety has remained unsuccessful in surpassing the Indian Theatre. No doubt – an actor who works in a cinema gets more money than a player of the stage but- the player of the stage gets more appreciation than the actor on the screen. The camera of a movie allows the compensation of a re-take to the actor whereas for the artist of a theatre no re-take is possible. His work demands more sincerity and higher efficiency which finally bring greater appreciation to him.

The tradition of Indian Drama is very old. It goes back to the Sanskrit Drama of ancient India. India being a large country with diverse cultures and regional languages has various traditions of form and matter, distinct and yet having many common factors of dramaturgy. Modern Indian drama is influenced not only by classical Sanskrit drama or local folk forms but also by western theatre following the establishment of British rule in India.

N. S. Dharan, an eminent writer of Indian writing in English writes "Drama in India has a long history". Girish Karnad says that the earliest extant play in India was written as early as A.D. 200. Dating to the days of Bhasa, Bhavabuti and Kalidasa, drama can boast of a rich and chequered history. The early plays were written in Sanskrit, based on the Vedas and the Upanishads. In fact, the Vedas and the Upanishads have never ceased to be sources of inspiration to man of letters both in India and abroad. Down the centuries, Indian drama has undergone various metamorphoses and it still continues to flourish in all regional languages. In regional languages it enjoys almost an equal status along with two other major literary genres, namely fiction and poetry. In Indian literature drama in English is yet to register an appreciable growth. By and large, plays written in regional languages dominate the Indian theatre. These plays are easily intelligible to the audiences. Actors too can easily improvise in them.

Several regional amateur theatres have also flourished from time to time. In the post-Independence period, performing arts were employed as an effective means of public enlightenment during the First-Five year plan (1951-54). As a result the National school of Drama was established under the directorship Alkhazi. Institutions for training in dramatics were founded in big cities. Drama departments started functioning in several universities. The annual Drama Festival was started in New Delhi by the Sangit Natak Akademi in 1954. With so much encouragement coming from so many quarters, drama began to flourish in the regional languages.

During the last few years, several plays, originally written in the regional languages, have been translated into English. Today, a sizeable number of such plays do exist. According to many academicians, it is necessary to incorporate these translations into the corpus of Indian English Literature as they also contribute an important component to it. Such translations of plays have forged an effective link between the East and the West the North and the South of India and contributed, in no small measure, to the growing harmony and richness of contemporary creative consciousness.

According to **Indranath Chaudhary**, when the sahitya Akademi was set up in 1954, Dr. S. Radhakrishnan spelt out its objective as the promotion of the unity of Indian literature, despite India's geographical, political, Social, and Linguistic diversities. Dr. Radhakrishnan gave a slogan to the Akademi that Indian literature is one, though written in many languages. It is in this context that the plays of Girish Karnad in Kannada, Mohan Rakesh in Hindi, Badal Sircar in Bengali and Vijay Tendulkar in Marathi occupy a unique place as pointed out by **Arundhati Banerjee** :

"In the 1960s four dramatisls from different regions of India writing in their own regional languages were said to have ushered modernity in to the sphere of Indian drama and theatre. They were Mohan Rakesh in Hindi, Badal Sircar in Bengali and Vijay Tendulkar in Marathi and Girish Karnad in Kannada. Rakesh's untimely death left his life's work incomplete, and Karnad has written only intermittently. Sircar, of course, has been almost as active as Tendulkar though his plays can be divided in to three distinct periods. Tendulkar, however, has not only been the most productive but has also introduced the greatest variations in his dramatic creations."

V. B. Deshpande rightly states, "Since the Independence – since 1950, to be precise – the name of Vijay Tendulkar has been in the forefront of the Marathi drama and stage. His personality both as man and writer is multifaceted. It has often been puzzling and curious with a big question mark on it. In the last 55 years he has written stories, novels, one – act plays, plays for children as well adults. Similarly he has done script6 writing and news paper columns as well. And in all these fields he has created an image of his own. Thus he is a creative writer with a fine sensibility and at the same time a contemplative and controversial dramatist. He has made a mark in the field of journalism also. Because of his highly individual viewpoint and vision of life and because of his personal style of writing he has made a powerful impression in the field of literature and drama, and has given the post-independence, Marathi drama a new idiom. By doing this he has put Marathi drama on the national and international Map."

The same indebtedness is expressed by **Arundhati Banerjee** "Vijay Tendulkar has been in the vanguard of not just Marathi but Indian theatre for almost forty years".He not only pioneered the experimental theatre movement in Marathi but also guided it."

While talking about contemporary Marathi Theatre **Dhyaneshwar Nadkarni** points out,

"Vijay Tendulkar leads the vanguard of the avant garde theatre that developed as a movement separate from the mainstream. Tendulkar and his colleagues were dissatisfied with the decadent professional theatre that characterized the Thirties and Forties. They wanted to give theatre a new form and therefore experimented with all aspects of it including content, acting décor and audience communication."

Chandrasekhar Barve expresses a similar opinion about Tendulkar's contribution to Marathi theatre,

"We can say with certainty that Tendulkar has guided Marathi drama that seemed to have lost its proper track, and has kept leading it for over two decades. His place and importance in this respect shall remain unique in the history of Marathi drama. There may be controversies regarding his greatness but his achievements are beyond question.

He has written 28 full length plays, 24 one-act plays, several middles, articles, editorials and 11 plays for children. In spite of his success in every genre, his versatility as a writer has been overshadowed by his fame as a dramatist since drama has been his forte.

Mr. Barve observes,
"His extra-dramatic writing also reveals his pure taste for drama which tries to capture the different tensions and through them, finds "dramatics" accurately".His one-act plays are more

experimental than his full-length plays. Most of them have been translated and produced in major Indian languages and some of them into English.

Vijay Tendulkar was born in **1928** at **Bombay** in **Maharastra**. He was born and brought up in Kandevali, a small lane in Girgaon. A lower middle class community dwelt. There and the males were mostly the shopkeepers and clerks. He was living in a typical chawl, in apartments of one room, kitchen, balcony and common toilets, so Tendulkar's upbringing in a lower middle class community provided him chance to perceive middle class minutely which helped him to portray its different shades on the stage.

His **father Mr. Dhondopant Tendulkar** was a head clerk at a British publishing firm called Longmans Green and company (Now Orient Longman). His **mother Mrs. Susheela Tendulkar** was a housewife. His father was a writer, director and actor of amateur Marathi plays. He didnot join the commercial drama company as formerly a career in the theatre was not honoured. Four years old Tendulkar used to go with his father to the rehearsals so he nurtured love for the theatre from his childhood. Tendulkar himself considers those rehearsals as a kind of "Magic show". Because like magic he saw the living beings change into characters. He saw with wonder the male performing the roles of woman by changing their voice and movements. He didn't have any exposure to other theatre except what his father staged.

Tendulkar had other **brother** named **Raghunath** and **sister Leela**. His two elder sisters died in infancy. He had two younger brothers but- he was the favourite child of his parents. He was sickly child and suffering from cough and asthmatic wheezing. So special care, protection and love were provided to this sickly boy by the parents for fear of losing him if not protected well. He was given the **pet name "Papia"** and above all he was known as a **"Mother's child"** being favourite of his mother. Emotionally he was more attached with his mother than his father. He remembers how his mother used to feed him forcefully.

Due to his unhealthy body the family servant used to take him to school. It was municipal school. As usual it had small dingy rooms with awful toilets and it had no playground and water at times. In the school also special attention was given to him as he belonged to somewhat well to do family. His teachers used to borrow story books from him and by becoming partial they left him alone at the examination. Thus he studied in an average Indian school, which has no basic facilities but he carries those moments in comparison with sophisticated school where he studied later in life. At 9 years of age he attended "Chikisaha samooha", where he found himself totally strange among the sophisticated children and spacious buildings.

Tendulkar surprisingly started his career as a **writer** at a very early stage of life. He wrote stories and essays when he was **6** years of age. His father was a writer, director and actor so creativity was inborn in him. The unpublished work of his father lay at home and little Tendulkar passed his time with books and had read novel and short stories of eminent writers so he grew up in a literary atmosphere. The seed had already been sown in little mind for literature and gradually it took the shape of huge tree.

He had never imagined himself to be a writer in his childhood. As a small child he wanted to be an engine driver or an acrobat in circus and dreamt of wondering from place to place astonishing the crowd by daredevil acts. He used to visit fairs and circus with his father which were like big fairyland for him. So childlike curiosity, interest and amazement surrounded him along with his keen interest in reading. Sunday and vacation had special attraction for him. On Sunday morning his father used to take him to a large bookshop of his friend used to buy books of his choice. In evening his father took him to chowpatty beach and they travelled in train from Charni Road to Colaba which attracted him a lot. During summer vacation the family used to go for Goa or to Port Ratnagiri.

Tendulkar remembers that his father was a strict disciplinarian, impractical, stubborn but an honest man. "To be honest is a disqualification in todays world" and so Mr. Dhondopant Tendulkar never got the honour of being honest and idealist. He never took bribes or extra fees. But he felt proud to be poor and was very much content with life. Due to this the later life of his father was miserable. The elder brother Raghunath quarrelled with him and left the home. His father was against the dowry system and so Tendulkar's sister Leela didn't get married and had to remain single. It seems that the father had never got family love due to certain principles.

Apart from the influence of the father, Raghunath, his brother also played formative influence on Tendulkar. His brother was a follower of Gandhi and Gandhian principles. He used to attend political congress meetings. The father wanted him to be active in studies but he went astray. He wanted to marry Hansa Wadkar which was unbearable for the idealist father and so the family separated from Raghunath and moved to Kolhapur. Tendulkar used to get gifts like pastries, sweets and pen from his brother. He used to go for English movies with his brother. But his brother died miserably due to alchoholic habit.

The later childhood of Tendulkar passed at Kolhapur – a princely state in Maharastra. At Kolhapur he made himself noticeable by his excellence in reciting English poems. When he was **11 years** old, he **wrote** and **directed** and **acted "Maya Bazaar".** This way, the journey of this veteran writer towards performing arts started. At Kolhapur his friend was the son of one prominent playwright named Na vi kulkarni, who shared the same literary interest with Tendulkar. He even worked as a **child artist** in **two Marathi** Films.

As a teenager, at the **age** of **13** the family shifted to Pune and he attended a new school. He believed that he might have completed matriculation but the **Quit India Movement** was in momentum and Tendulkar was one of those who obeyed Gandhi's call to boycott the school. He started taking part in campaign against Britishers and he used to attend the early morning meetings without informing his parents. At the **age** of **14** while attending such meeting, he **was arrested** and the family came to know about Tendulkar's active participation in freedom fighting. Again he attended the school but now he started bunking the classes and developed the habit of spending the monthly fees of the **school** in watching English films. The visuals had a good impact on him. This exposure to the theatre at an early age has had its strong influence on him as a **successful** dramatist. He says in an interview, "As a school boy I had watched the Hollywood films playing in my hometown, not once, but each one over and over again. I still remember the visuals, not the dialogues which I didn't understand. A more conscious education in what the visual could do came when I worked with the Rangayan Theatre group in Bombay, but watching Marcel Marceau from the last seat in the last row was an enthralling experience. Not a single word was uttered, but so much was expressed. After that I wrote mimes for quite a while. I felt the visual had unlimited possibilities, the word was useless. But I am a playwright, words are my tools, I had to use them." Apart from Films he denoted his time at the city library in reading which helped him a lot during his career as a journalist. But his father was disappointed seeing the poor prospect of Tendulkar.

At Pune, Tendulkar found the **Role Model** of his life – **Dinkar BalKrishna Mokashi,** a radio mechanic but a good writer. He led a very simple life and Tendulkar was impressed by his personality and the informality of his writing style. His other **Role Model** was **Vishnu Vinayak Bokil,** a teacher and a writer.

Tendulkar liked his light hearted, jovial and exuberant style. He remembered one incident of the school when Mr. Vinayak asked the students to look at the names of rank holders of the school on the board and asked, "Where are those top rankers now? Does anyone know?"Then he said that the students should pass the exam as the parents pay the fees but the marks they get were not everything. He advised them to develop their personality in other directions also. It worked as a boosting to the teen Tendulkar to look beyond the school. Later on, as a writer Tendulkar dedicated one of his book to this school teacher Mr. Vinayak.

At 16, Tendulkar **left the school** for good. He had no friends and no any communication with his parents. He wanted to talk! But with whom! He had to talk with himself! And he put all his dialogues with his own self on paper through various forms-poems stories, film scripts and at this stage of his life his writing acquired a conscious motivation.

At the age of **22** he wrote his **First full length original play "Grihastha"** which flopped like anything and he took an oath that he would never write a play in life and to his surprise he has written **28 full length** plays as well as he has been **working actively** in the theatre world for the last **45 years.**

He always considers himself a writer first and a playwright after words. About his love for writing he writes,

"The point is more than a playwright, I consider myself to be a writermeaning I loved to indulge in the physical process of writing. I enjoy this process even when there is nothing to be said.

Give me a piece of paper any paper and pen and I shall write as naturally as a bird flies or a fish swims. Left to myself, I scribble. And I never get tired of writing… Especially when I write in my mother tongue i.e. Marathi. Writing gives me a pleasure which has no substitute. However, tired I am physically or mentally, the moment I pick up the pen and begin running it on a paperany piece of paper I feel good I feel refreshed I feel as if I am born again. Writing by itself is a luxury for me. When I write, I forget myself, I forget my anxieties…"

He has been writing in different roles by using different mediums. He was **journalist**. He had been **sub-editor** and executive editor in journals and assistant editor of a daily. He used to write editorials with the information received from the second hand sources. This filled him with great dissatisfaction. He says,

"It started with my journalistic dissatisfaction but it grew into much bigger proportions in the sense that it became a matter of conscience as a human being. I became restless."

The violence, the oppression and the exploitation in the society that he witnessed made him restless. And journalism could not offer him a viable solution for his mental agitation. But it does shape his dramatic career. **Gowri Ramnarayan**, therefore points out: "With his exposure to Marathi theatre from childhood, and journalistic background Vijay Tendulkar turned contemporary socio-political situations into explosive drama."

His desire was to start a daily newspaper column and he enjoyed **writing a column** for **six months** in 1993, when Babri

Masjid was destroyed. And during those six months he didn't write anything but only enjoyed column writing. He well remembered that during his journalistic days he sometimes wrote for astrology column, when the 'official' astrologer did not reach in time and he enjoyed in forecasting bright future for the unknown readers of the column. As a writer he found good fun in playing the **role** of **an astrologer**.

Being versatile he can put himself in any role. During the period of struggle he did **Ghost writing** with full knowledge that his name would not appear and become known to the readers. He took it as a role with its own "character". His inner personality as a writer underwent a natural change to suit the role. Along with his job in a newspaper he started writing short story and play and even Ghost writing for additional income. His writing developed according to the demands of the roles. He also worked as a **Public Relation Officer** in an industry and wrote copy for add-agencies. He **translated** American Books for the united information services and wrote **scripts** for non-descript Government Documentaries. He played different roles in order to earn his livelihood but his writing practice has brought perfection in writing skill.

Vijay Tendulkar, as a sensitive, sensible and responsible citizen, could not quieten his agitated conscience with his journalistic career. So he left journalism when he received Nehru Fellowship for the 1973-75. During this period, he travelled extensively throughout India and saw directly all kinds of violence.

From this experience, he infers:

"Unlike communists I don't think that violence can be eliminated in a classless society, or, for that matter, in any society. The spirit of aggression is something that the human being is born with. Not that it's bad. Without violence man would have turned into a vegetable."So he perceived both the positive and negative faces of violence.

Regarding ideology he says,

"I do not align myself to any political ideology.......I do have my sympathies with the left"He does not subscribe to any ideology in his plays. Nor does he write for commercial purpose. Moreover, in the words of **Mr. Barve,**

"Tendulkar's plays helped to refine Marathi drama that was so far polluted by propaganda for political awakening and social reforms, cheap and vulgar entertainment". Tendulkar does not subscribe to any particular political Ideologies, as they, including Marxism, are unable to understand the complex human situation and to suggest any viable solution to our Hydra-headed problems. Yet he does not lack political awareness.

He says to **Gowri Ramnarayan** in an interview,

"I had a political background, I was involved in the 1942 movement.Journalism developed my political sense, curiosity for instance ....naturally this got in my writing."

He was actively associated with civil liberties movements in Maharashtra. All this shows his great concern for his country and society. He is a realist and refuses to be fooled by romantic concepts of reforms and movements. He exposed the flaws and the inevitable failure of unrealistic reforms and movements in his plays.

Mr. Tendulkar considers himself as an **actor-writer** and himself acted on the stage during his apprentice days in the theatre but did not find it as exciting as writing. He was an actor on the stage of his creative mind. According to him he acts as he writes in his mind he emotes the **lives** of the character as he writes. They are not written words but a total and spontaneous expression of the mind and the personality of the character which includes not only the words but also the eloquent silence in between the words-broken sentences, the subtle emphasis on certain words, even the pitch of the voice, the gestures of the hands. He can 20 visualize the position of the characters on the stage – the total composition of the scene and even the lighting. Thus he acted their speech, behavior patterns and their ways of looking at things. So he believes he can act better than others because he has acted his play out when he wrote the play. **Mr. Tendulkar** was basically **a man of theatre**, which he had inherited from his father and eldest brother. He had a curiosity for this performing art and subconscious and unquenched desire to explore the magic and beauty of this form. His love for the theatre continued as he wrote plays at school, acted in plays, watched it, discussed it and for the last 45 years he was in the world of theatre. He believes that performing art is addictive.

He writes,

"You can learn the "grammar" but art is not mere grammar. It is an expression it provides endless learning by experiments, by committing mistakes."

He remembered that at a very early stage of his life he had developed curiosity for people and consciously noted the speech habits of people, their manners and personal peculiarities. He gives an expression to it in his writing so some of his characters are related to certain living persons. He believed that the creative process is complicated process. The characters would appear in utter chaos till he conceives it. He could never write a play with only idea or theme in mind but he needed character first with him. He writes,

"I could not proceed to write a play unless I saw my characters as real life people, unless I could see them moving doing things by themselves, unless I heard them emoting, talking to each other, I was never able to begin writing my play only with an idea or a theme in mind. I had to have my characters first with me ...." Thus, they are not puppets but living persons of distinction.

About the structuring of his play he said he had never attended any courses for this skill but he had learnt it by trial and error method which is very costly. He wrote that one has to own money in experimental theatre. No one sponsors the play and by the time the players correct the mistakes they are doing the last show of the play. For him, the Rehearsal Hall had become the learning ground. In absence of theatrical devices the inner mechanism of a play with its positive and negative points were laid open and he learnt a lot from these brain- storming rehearsal sessions. Apart from experimenting in the theatre, watching rehearsals he used to see play every day once, twice or thrice in one day. He did not bother whether the play is good or bad but it helped him in internalizing the techniques of playwriting – especially the structuring of the play.

He learnt a lot by watching films because a film also has to have a structure. Even the **concerts** of **classical music impressed** him though he did not know its grammar but classical music has its strict rules and regulations. The **reading** of **the poems** also supplied him the knowledge about compact structure and a form. The visit to the **Art Galleries** made him aware about the rhythm, form and structure in good painting. Apart from all these **Peter Brook's** Book (Master Craftsman in the art of Theatre) taught him the foremost principles of theatre world that all visual art including the art of the theatre, have one thing in common- The space, and it is the skill of the dramatist that how meaningfully and ingeniously he fills the space.

Arundhati Banerjee says,

"Tendulkar's first major work that set him apart from previous generation Marathi playwrights was *Manus Navache Bel (An Island called Man)* (1955). His dramatic genius was cutout for the newly emerging, experimental Marathi theatre of the time. His direct association with Rangayan at this point of his career and continous interaction with such theatre personalities as Vijaya Mehta, Arvind and Sulabha Despande, Kamalakar Sarang Madhav Vatve and Damoo Kenkre provided new impetus for creative faculties. Thus Manus Navache Bel was closely followed by a spate of plays (1958). *Madhlya Bhinti (The walls Between) Chimnicha Ghar Hota Menacha (Nest of wax) (1958) Mee Jinklo Mee Harlo (I won, I lost) (1963) Kavlanchi Shala (school for crows) (1963) and Sari Ga Sari (Rain o Rain) (1964)* which would chart the course of avant-grade Marathi theatre during the next few years. There seems to be a consistency of theme and treatment in them despite the apparently desperate nature of their subjects. In all these early plays, Tendulkar is concerned with the middle class individual set against the backdrop of a hostile society."

Most of Tendulkar's plays are in the naturalistic writing. However, his Ghashiram Kotwal is in the folk tradition while his last two plays *Niyatioya Bailala (To Hell with Destiny)* and *Safar (The Tour)* emplay fantasy. The play **"Silence! The court is in session"** (1967) made him the centre of a general controversy. He has already been called the angry young man of the Marathi theatre. He was considered a rebel against the established values of a fundamentally orthodox society **Encounter in** Umbugland (1974) is a political allegory (1971) **The Vultures** shocked the conservative sections of Marathi people with its naturalistic display of cupidity, sex, and violence. **Sakharam Binder** (1972) is probably Tendulkar's most intensely naturalistic play and shocked the conservative society even more than **The Vultures**. In

Ghashiram Kotwal (1972) he moves from the naturalistic writing in to the folk tradition, it explains the power game that are found in Indian politics. **Kamala** (1981) is based on **a** real life incident reported in The Indian Express by Ashwin sarin. Kanyadaan is also one of the controversial play and branded as anti – Dalit play. It actually tries to show how our romantic idealism fails.

He wrote his plays in Marathi, First, he influenced Marathi theatre and guided it. Later, his impact extended to other Indian languages as his plays were translated into them. Tendulkar perceived the realities of the human society without any reconceived notions, reacted to them as a sensitive and sensible human being and wrote about them in his plays as a responsible writer. He never wrote to win a prize or an award.

He says,

"I have written about my own experience and about what I have seen in others around me. I have been true to all this and have not cheated my generation. I did not attempt to simplify matters and issues for the audience when presenting my plays, though that would have been easier occupation. Sometimes my plays jolted society out of its stupor and I was punished. I faced this without regrets. It is an old habit with me to do what I am told not to do. My plays could not have been anything else. They contain my perceptions of society and its value and I cannot write what I do not perceive".

In his plays he deals with the issues of gender inequality, social inequality, power games, self alienation, sex and violence.

His characters are very much real. They are neither completely good nor completely bad. He liberated Marathi stage from the tyranny of conventional theatre with its mild doses of social and political satire for purpose of pure entertainment.

Mr. M. Sarat Babu writes,

"Vijay Tendulkar portrays the contemporary society and the predicament of man in it with a special focus on the morbidity in his plays, which remind us of Nietzche's words "the disease called man" and also Freud's description of human civilization as "a universal neurosis". His plays touch almost every aspect of human life in the modern world and share the disillusionment of the post modern intellectuals, however they seem to highlight three major issues : gender, power and violence."

Vijay Tendulkar devoted his life for the world of theatre as he says ,

"What I like about those years is that they made me grow as a human being. And theatre which was my major concern has contributed to this in a big way. It helped me to analyse my own life and the lives of others. It led me to make newer and newer discoveries in the vast realm of the human mind which still defies all available theories and logic. It is like an everintriguing puzzle or a jungle which you can always enter but has no way out…"Such a prolific and versatile writer has been felicitated with many awards and honours like

1. The Maharashtra State Government Award (1956, 1969 and 1973)

2. The Sangeet Natak Akademi Award (1971)

3. The Filmfare Award (script writer) (1980,1983)

4. The Padmabhushan (1984)

5. The Saraswati Samman (1993)

6. The Kalidas Samman (1999)

7. The Maharashtra Gaurav Puraskar (1999)

8. The Jansthan Award (1999)

9. Katha Chudamani Award (2001)

This legendary theatre man passed away on **19th May, 2008**. He was suffering from Myasthenia Gravis, a neuromuscular disease. He died at the age of 80 in a private hospital at Pune where he was hospitalized since 10th April, 2008.Shirish Prayag, Director of Prayag Hospital stated,"At the time of his demise he was extremely calm and quiet. There was an expression of contentment on his face. His face did not reflect any pain."

Mr. Prayag stated that the family members had discussed the possibility of eye donation but it was decided that since Tendulkar had not expressed such a wish it would be improper to do so. Tendulkar who was in Pune, since he was last discharged from hospital had refused to go back to Mumbai."

According to his wish his last rites were performed at the Vaikanth electric crematorium and prominent theatre and film personalities including Mohan Agashe, Satish Alekar, Haider Ali, Amruta Subhash, Amol Palekar and Atul Pethe, university of Pune vice-chanceller Narendra Jadhav paid last tribute to Tendulkar at the crematorium.

- ➢ **Condolence Messages on Vijay Tendulkar's DeathPresident Pratibha Patil** said in her condolence message "Vijay Tendulkar was not only an acknowledged figure in Indian literature but also helped Marathi and all of Indian theatre attain recognition at the international level."

- ➢ **Prime Minister Manmohan** Singh in a condolence message to Tendulkar's family said, "his strog espousal of women's empowerment and the empowerment of the downtrodden has shaped public consciousness in post independence India."

- ➢ **Leader of Opposition L K Advani** also paid glowing tributes to Tendulkar. He said the playwright was an outstanding writer who gave Marathi theatre a national and international profile."His place, many of which were translated into Hindi and other Indian Languages, were both creative and carried a strong social message,"

- ➢ **Maharashtra Chief Minister Vilasrao Deshmukh** also condoled the death of eminent playwright Vijay Tendulkar.In his condolence message, Deshmukh said: "The nation has lost the literary genius and dramatist par excellence. With Tendulkar's death an eventful era has come to an end."

- Noted film **director Shyam Benegal** said : "Tendulkar was one of the greatest playwright of Indian theatre in the last 50 years. Tendulkar wrote screenplay of my films "Nishant" and "Manthan". I respected his creativity and admired him as a human being." "He was a senior professional form our field and his contribution to the Indian theatre was immense," Benegal added.

- **Film director Govind Nihlani** said : "Tendulkar brought modernity to Marathi theatre. He pioneered a paradigm shift in the vision of looking at society and reflecting it through theatre and cinema."

- **Bollywood superstar Mr. Amitabh Bachchan** said : " Vijay Tendulkar was a strong and fearless writer and a great mind. I am deeply saddened to hear the news of his passing away." Amitabh was full of admiration for the man who re-wrote many rules of stage writing. "In today's world it is difficult and though to take a committed stand and pursue it. Vijay Tendulkarji did. And that was his strength. At times this stand is the solitary voice of reason often misunderstood but seldom wrong."

- **Amol Palekar said**: "His death is a loss to theatre and literature. wonder whether this losss will ever be recovered. I am glad I could do my share of archiving his entire body of work for the younger generation when my wife Sandhya Gokhale and I organized a Ten Festival in 2006 which went on for a week.

List of Vijay Tendulkar's Works :

One Act :

Thief Police

Ratra Ani Itar Ekankika (1957)

Chitragupta, Aho Chitragupta (1958)

Ajgar Ani Gandharv (1966)

Bhekad Ani Itar Ekankika (1969)

Ekekacha

Andher Nagari

Collection of Stories :

Kaachpatre (1957)

Dwandwa (1961)

Gane (1966)

Phulpakharu (1970)

Essays :

Kovil Unhe (1971)

Rat Rani (1971)

Phuge Savanache (1974)

Ram Prakar (1994)

Children's Plays :

Ithe Bale Miltat (1960)

Patlachya Poriche Lageen (1965)

Chimna Bandhto Bangla (1966)

Chambhar Chauksiche Natak (1970)

Novels :

Kadambari

Katha Eka Vyathechi : Henry James

Nave Ghar : Nave Ayushya : Grace Jordan

Prempatre : Henry James

Aage Barho : G L Letham (1958)

Gele Te Divas (1958)

Devanchi Manse

Amhu Harnhar Nahi: L E Wilder

Ranphul : S L Arora (1963)

Chityachya Magawar : W W Tiberg

Clarke (1957)

Humour :

Karbhareen : Doroothy Von Doren

Biography :

Dayechi Devta : H D Wiloston

To Aamchayasathi Ladhla (Roosevelt) : K O Pear

Film Script (Marathi)

Samana
Sinhasan
Umbartha
Akriet
22 June 1897

Film Script (Hindi)

Nishant
Manthan
Akrosh
Ardha Satya
Aaghat

Play	Original Title	Original Author	Original Language	Institution	Director	First Show	Pub.	Yrs.
Adhe Adhure	Adhe Adhure	Mohan Rakesh	Hindi	Theatre Unit	Satyadev Dube	11th Jan. 1970	Popular	1971
Lincolon Che Akherche Divas	Last Days of Lincolon	Mark Doran	English	-	-	-	Majestic	1964
Lobh Nasava hi Vinanti	Hasty Heart	John Patrick	English	Rangayan	Arvind Deshpande	-	Parchure	-
Tughaluq	Tughaluq	Girish Karnad	Kannda	Avishkar	Arvind Deshpande	17th Aug. 1971	Niklanth	1971
Vasarach Akra	A street Car Named Desire	Tenesse Williams	English	-	-	-	Popular	1966

Dramatic Works

Title	Institute	Director	First Show	Publication
Ghrihasth (The House Holder)	Mumbai marathi Sahitya Sangha, Drama Wing	Damu Kenkare	1955 Exact date not known	-
Sjro,amt (The rich)	Bharatiya vidya bhavan kala kendra	Vijaya Mehta	12th Dec. 1955	1955
Manus navache Bet (An Island Called man)	Lalit kala Kendra	Damu kenkare	28th Oct. 1956	1956
Madhalya Bhinti (Middle Walls)	Best Art Section	Nandkumar Rawate	4th Nov. 1958	1958
Chimanicha Ghar Hota menacha (The Wax House of the Sparrow	Rangmancha	Vijaya Mehta	27th Dec. 1959	1960
Mi Jinkalo (I Won, I lost)	Rangayan	Vijaya Mehta	20th Oct. 1963	1963
Kavlyanchi Shala (School for Crows)	Rangayan	Vijaya Mehta	5th Dec. 1963	1964
Sarga Sari (Drizzle O Drizzle)	Mumbai Marathi Sahitya Sangh, Drama wing	Arvind Deshpande	18th May 1964	1964
Ek Hatti Mulagi (An obstinate Girl)	Kala Vaibhav	Almram Bhende	21th Nov. 1966	1968

Shatata Court Chalu Ahe (Silence! The Court is in Session)	Rangayan	Arivind Deshpande	28th Dec. 1967	1968
Jhala Anant Hanumant	-	Arvind Deshpande	-	1968
Dambdwipacha Mukbala (An Encounter in Umbugland)	Rangayan	Arvind Deshpande	10th Dec. 1969	1974
Gidhade (The Vulture)	Theatre Unit	Shriram lagu	29th May 1970	1971
Ashi Pakhare Yeti (So Come Birds)	Progressive Dramatic Association, Pune	Jabbar Patel	26th Nov. 1970	1970
Sakharam Binder	Welcome theatres	Kamalar Sarang	10th mar. 1972	1972
Bhalya kaka	Natya Mandar	Arvind Deshpande	5th April 1972	1974
Gharate Amuche Chan (Nice is our Nest)	Welcome Theatre	kamalakar Sarang	28th Oct. 1972	1973
Ghashiram Kotwal	Progressive Dramatic Association, Pune	Jabbar Patel	16th Dec. 1972	1973
Baby	nateshwar	Kamalakar Sarang	29th Aug. 1976	1975
Bhai Murarrao	Theatre Academy Pune	Mohan gokhale	13th Sept. 1977	1975

29

Pahije Jatiche	-	Arvind Deshpande	-	1976
Mitrachi Goshta (A Friend's Story)	Bhumika	Vinay Aapte	15th Aug. 1981	1982
kamala	Kala Rang	kamalakar Sarang	7th Aug. 1981	1982
Kanyadan	INT	Sadashiv Amarapurkar	12th Feb. 1983	1983
Vithala	INT	Sadashiv Amarapurkar	22nd May 1985	1985
Chiranjeev Saubhagya kanshini	Abhishek	Kamalakar Sarang	14th Dec. 1991	-
Safar	Avishkar	Sulbha Deshpande	6th Jan. 1992	-
Niyatichya bailala Ho (To Hell with the Bull of the Fate)	-	-	-	-

2. GHASHIRAM KOTWAL : AN OVERVIEW

Ghashiram Kotwal is set in eighteenth century Pune at the time of the Peshwa rule. The play features the Peshwa's chancellor Nana Phadnavs and when it was first staged it came up against a lot of criticism of or showing the revered Nana's character in a derogatory light. According to Tendulkar:

This is not a historical play. It is a story, in prose, verse, music and dance set in a historical era. Ghashirams are creations of socio-political forces which know no barriers of time and place. Although based on a historical legend, I have no intention of commentary on the morals, or lack of them, of the Peshwa, Nana Phadnavis or Ghashiram. n e moral of this story, if there is any, may be looked for elsewhere.

('Introduction,' Ghashiram Kotwal, 4)

History has been transformed into a lively situation full of theatrical potential rate Nana He is described as 'secretive, exclusive and often vindictive, his exacting and stern. methods, his

insistence more upon the form than the essence in a thousand and one matters of administration, did in the long run harm to the Maratha State'. Nana was born on 12th Feb, 1742 and lived to be 58 years one month. He married several wives, of whom the names of nine are available. His last wife named Julbai who became a widow by his death, was then nine years of age. In the writers" note to Vasant Deo's Hindi translation, Tendulkar says :

In my view Ghashiram Kotwal indicates a particular social situation which is neither old nor new. It is beyond time and space. Therefore 'Ghashiram' and Nana Phadnavis are are also beyond space and time'.(Web citation)

The story is about Ghashiram, a Brahman from the North, who comes to eighteenth century Poona. It was at that time that the Peshwa's chief minister Nana Phadnavis ruled supreme. Implicated in a false charge of theft, Ghashiram is insulted and humiliated by the

Poona Bhrahmans and he vows to take revenge. His moment comes when the ageing lecherous Nana takes a fancy to his beautiful-young daughter Lalita Gauri. He sacrifices hisdaughter's virtue to the Nana's lust and manages to become the Kotwal of Poona. Now heunleashes a reign of terror on the Brahmans.

His cruelty crosses all limits and the death of 22 innocent Brahmans results in his downfall and leads to his ignominious end when he is stoned to death. The Nana who has used Ghashiram's daughter and discarded her when he moves on to frees pastures goes scot free. After Ghashiram's death, he announces public rejoicing for three days. The play is asatire on a society which shields. The powerful and the corrupt and punishes people like

Ghashiram. Justice is seen to be done, and the equilibrium of society seems to be restored.The personality clash between the Nana and Ghashiram may appear to be the theme at the surface level but Tendulkar has examined the relationship between religion, caste,sexuality and violence to expose the structures of power that maintain the status quo.

Tendulkar is concerned about the politics of power and its various implications. According to Samik Bandhopadhyay, 'In Ghashiram, power is defined horizontally in terms of individuals against individuals from humiliation to eventual victimization.' (Collected Plays in Translation:Vijay Tendulkar. 5.)

The play begins with a religious hymn and the popular gods dancing on stage. Thissets the context against which the drama unfolds itself. The Brahmans go to Bavannakhani to see the dancing girls and say they are going 'to the temple' to give a sermon on 'Vishwamitra and Menaka'. They justify their decadence by comparing Bavannakhani to holy Mathura. The 'abhanga' or devotional song is often sung with the 'Iavani' or love song in his play. Scenes of violence and cruelty are alternated with devotional song. When Nana tries to seduce Gauri in front of the statue of the holy Ganapati, he simply dismisses her fears saying 'That all holy

Ganapati? The maker of Good? Look, he has two wives. One on this side, one on that side'.(GK,8) Further on in the play when Gauri is dead and the distraught Ghashiram confronts the Nana and accuses him of his daughter's death, the latter reassures him: 'He – the Omnipresent - He makes everything happen ...... We are merely instruments ......' He then urges him to 'forget whats happened. All merges into the Ganga Thou shall not grieve over what is gone. The Vedas have said that' (GK 44) It is a case of the devil citing scriptures to suit his purpose? Religion becomes a useful alibi in covering people's misdeeds. By invoking religion, all kinds of evils are glossed and even sanctified. Rituals are encouraged to fill the pockets of the greedy Brahmans. Moreover, their position as the 'twice born' is reinforced by the prevalence of the caste system.

3. THE 18th CENTURY POWER POLITICS AND ITS CONTEMPORARY RELEVANCE

Longman Dictionary of contemporary English defines "POLITICS'' as the art or science of government and "POWER POLITICS" as the system of gaining an adventage for one's country in international politics by the use or show of armed force instead of by peaceful argument.

To indulge in politics is inborn instinct of man. The scriptures of the world testify it. In the old Testament of the Bible in Genesis, our ancestors Adam and Eve play politics with God and commit the sin of disobedience by tasting the forbidden fruit in order to get God-like quality. Even their younger child Cain murdered his elder brother Abel to get the favour of God. The Hindu scriptures "Mahabarat" and "Ramayan" also display the game of shrewd power politics.

In **Ramayan** Kaikaiyi and Manthara symbolise the game of power politics. In **Mahabharat**, Duryodhan and Shakuni with their shrewd mind immortalize the word power politics. And even Lord Krishna had to play power politics in order to defeat "Adharm". So power politics is associated with the race of man.

www.southindpress.org defines Power politics,

"On the level of international politics, power can take many forms from moral suasion to the carrot of economic benefits to the stick of sanctions or military force. "Power politics" is one of the most equivocal terms in the lexicon of international affairs. In common usage, including that of politicians it often is value-laden, usually in a negative sense. It implies using coercion – force or threats of force – to impose one's will upon others. Thus one can define power politics both as a term commonly used in political rhetoric and a theoretical description of how states interact in pursuit of their interests in the international arena. In American English it usually means politics based primarily on coercion rather that on cooperation, whether that coercion be military or economic."

So, those who are attached with the government or the rulers know or learn the game of power of politics in order to be on the throne. Even the people never raise their voice if their interests are served and the world goes on. Consciously or unconsciously the people also become the part of power politics.

Shanta Gokhale writes

"Tendulkar wanted to make a serious political statement in Ghashiram Kotwal. That was why he wrote the play, not to vent his spleen against Brahmins, as many Brahmins thought, nor to desecrate the sanctity of the stage with lurid depiction of lasciviousness, nor rake in money by entertaining audiences with song and dance and a scandalous legend about a historical figure. Its reception by many as a brilliantly mounted entertaining spectacle upset the liberal social moralist. This, more than anything else, links Tendulkar with most significant of his predecessons on the Marathi stage – playwrights who wanted to force their society to look at and judge itself in all its aspects, socio, political, moral and personal."

Shanta Gokhale – excerpt from Shanta Gokhale's playwright at the center! Marathi drama from 1843 to present published by Seagull Books, Calcutta.

Tendulkar himself has agreed that his play is primarily "A study of the power game." His choice of subject itself indicates this. Tendulkar said that Ghashiram Kotwal was not a historical play and he had merely used some historical anecdotes and incidents to project the contemporary caste politics and power game in which women have been used. He explained "History interests me only in so far as it relates to my period and the situation around me."

Commenting on the form and the theme of the play, **Girish Karnad** explains clearly the contemporary relevance of the play in the **Introduction to his Three plays.**

"In his Ghashiram Kotwal, Tendulkar uses, Dashavatara, a traditional semi-classical form, to investigate a contemporary political problem, the emergence of "demon" in public. These demons are initially created by political leaders for the purpose of their own power games but ultimately go out of control and threaten to destroy their own creators. It is a theme recurrent in Indian mythology: the demon made indestructible by the boon of gods and then turning on gods themselves. (A decade after the play was written, in Punjab sant Bhindranwale and Mrs. Indira Gandhi is example of re-enaction of the theme in real life in horrifying detail). Therefore, unless we understand the power game in the play, we are likely to miss the theme and to agree with Veena NobelDass who says "The central weakness of the play is that Ghashiram has been provided with too explicit reason for his conversion form man to monster."

The play is an ironical commentary on our socio-political set up. Tendulkar could find a parallel in the history of Peshwa Empire and thereby suggest that such circumstances are not confined to a particular era but are seen in all times and discovered its contemporary relevance. When we see the end of one Ghashiram we presume that it is the end of all Ghashirams but the fact is that the emergence of Ghashirams is a universal phenomenon. Ghashirams grow and prosper as and when they get identical socio-political situations in our society. In this context Samik Bandopadhyay's observation is quite significant.

"Nana needs Ghashiram, and Ghashiram needs Nana, but in the shifting game of power, it is only a temporary adjustment that Nana exploits as long as necessary and can drop unceremoniously the moment it has served its purpose." Let's see how the evils in contemporary power politics are represented through 18th century reign of Peshwas.

The period from 1761 to 1818 was critical for the Maratha empire. But in such critical period one brain shines and when it fades the Maratha Empire starts declining. And the name of that man is Nana Phadnavis. His whole life is like an interesting novel.

Nana Phadnavis Balaji Janardan Bhanu (12 February 1742 – 13 March 1800) became Phadnavis (administrator) at the age of fourteen by hereditary right at the death of his father.

He did not have any experience of war or physical strong body. But, yes in the game of intellect he used to defeat everyone. His intellectual capacity can be compared with Chanakya. Through shrewd strategies he was able to defeat Britishers.

In the reign of Madhava Rao two youngmen came on the surface. They were – Mahadaji Shinde and Nana Phadnavis. Nana was a true patriot. Madhava Rao, Peshwa died in 1772 and a period of struggle started for Nana. Madhava Rao's brother Narayana Rao became the Peshwa but Rughunath killed him by treachery and became the Peshwa. Nana's devotion towards Peshwas made him restless and he fought with Raghunath and made Narayana Rao son Savai Madhava Rao the Peshwa. In his life career Nana phadnavis

- Fought & defeated the Britishers
- Defeated Haider Ali
- Controlled selfish landlords & Maratha officials
- Fought with Tipu Sultan

The war between Britishers & Marathas and treaty at Salbai.

Great victory in making Savai Madhava Rao as the new Peshwa and that too without shedding a single drop of blood through his sharp intellect, political strategy and statesmanship.

He was a shrewd statesman and he retained his power till his death. He had nine wives and no children.

Nana was a cult hero, who was worshipped as hero by Marathas. His flaws were ignored by the people, Being blind to their hero's treachery, they were only too ready to stone to death their Kotwal when their Phadnavis asked them to do so. However, it was this aspect of Phadnavis' character that Tendulkar chose to highlight. He even made Ghashiram, the Kotwal of Pune in exchange of his daughter. This shady aspect of Maratha's hero created great uproars in Pune where the play was first staged. The play which was staged by Bharat Natya Mandir Pune in Dec. 1972 was stopped by the president of Progressive Dramatic Association after 19 performances finding it controversial. The main reason behind the ban was.

N.S.Dharan writes,

"This deglamorization of a cult hero caused disquiet among Poonites who came down heavily upon the producer, director and actors of the "play". In Act I of the play Sutradhar announces the entry of Nana. At night, the life begins at Pune The city is dominated by Brahmins and Nana and the Brahmins, go to Bavannakhani where Gulabi, a courtesan, entertains Nana and his followers with dance and song. The degeneration of the class in power is evoked brilliantly when the sutradhar tells.

> The night progresses
> The night progresses
> The night progresses
> And the peshwas chief Minister,
> Nana of the nine courta
> Nana of the wealth AND 'POWER'
> NANA OF Bhadnavis
> To Gulabi's place proceeds.

Thus Nana and his subjects make most of their power and indulge in all kinds of indecent activities obsessed with unbridled sex. Nana neglects his duties. The society is rotten as the Brahmins who belong to the higher strata, behave as low men. They are the protectors of religion and scripture but they, themselves make the place immoral. Being self possessive they seek pleasure in the company of other women and fail to know what their women actually want. Ironically the women are equally corrupt. They wish to enjoy themselves as much as their men do as is clear from their solicitation of the Maratha paramours in the absence of their spouses. It is this immorality on the part of men and women which is typical of the modern society and stifles the springs of genuine human love. The Brahmins are unfaithful not only to their wives but also to their master using religion as a cover to hide their misdeeds. The hypocrisy of the Brahmins is brought out in thin attribution of sacredness to their immoral acts. They regard Bavannakhani the most sought after red light area as "Mathura Avatarli" associated with Lord Krishna. This reflects the weight of irreverence towards religious institutions which, built to uphold their right to superiority are transformed into centres of exploitation of the needy. Here the "kirtan" turns in to "Lavani". It reminds the contemporary evils attached with religion Recently in the newspaper and on T.V. it is reported that during "Gokal Ashtami" and "Ramlila" instead of "Bhajan – kirtan" some dancers – danced on filmy songs and the audience at the temple enjoyed it a lot without guilt, at Mathura and Kashi.

In Gujarat "Navratri" has become an occasion of obscenity instead of "Devotion". Nine – Nights have become an occasion for the younger generation to enjoy freedom in the name of "Mataji". Even the "Garaba" tradition of "Ma" has gone and filmi songs and Re-mixes have entered in the ground of temple. It provides the best opportunity for the girls to expose their body through their traditional "chaniya choli". This contemporary deterioration of religion is best depicted by Tendulkar through Bavannakhani.

In fact Tendulkar seems to suggest that "the operation of religiosity, sexuality, and deputationist politics serve as devices of power. Shanta Gokhale writes,

The juxtaposition of Bavannakhani, Pune's red light district (Bavannakhani means fifty two rooms), with Mathura where Krishna danced, sang and played with the cow girls, underlines the hypocrisy of the Brahmins who pray piously by day and play lasciviously by night – It is at this point that Nana is introduced. He comes "Carrying a silver headed cane, wearing a string of mogra flowers round his wrist and dancing to the beat of the song." The cane indicates riches and power, the string of flowers, sensuality, and the dancing, a surrender to the pursuit of pleasure. Nana has joined the dancers in the courtesan's room, suddenly he sprains his foot. In great pain, he dances a few steps on one leg. The Sutradhar asks a string of onomatopoetically rhymed questions about why Nana is limping How did it happen? Is the first straight question where did he fall? Is the second non-so-straight question because of the metaphorical association of falling. The third question suggests three different ways of falling, each hinting that the fall is the result of Nana's being where he ought not to have been. The final question literally translated is "Did his foot fall crooked?" making the double-entendres quite obvious, as "foot falling crooked" is a euphemism for illicit sexual adventure. So Nana hopping around on one leg becomes the visual incarnation of lechery. The image is transformed into one of power and patronage with the idea of the patronage-seeker's " bootlicking" built in the outsider, Ghashiram, waiting for a chance to find a legitimate position in the rich city of Pune. While working for the courtesan, Ghashiram sees his opportunity in Nana's predicament. He hurries forward and offers his bent back for Nana's sprained foot. Nana accepts the offer with gratitude and soon enquires who the man under his foot is and offers necklace to him."

So, Ghashiram earns the favour of Nana but the wrath of the Brahmins. The Brahmins regard him as a threat to their existence so they try to turn him out of their society. Ghashiram knows that Nana is a womanizer and can do anything for the sheer company of a woman. As such, he plans to please Nana by using his own daughter as bait to obtain a position in Nana's court.

Nana meets Ghashiram's daughter at a religious ceremony and is infatuated by her. It is described by the playwright thus:

Nana Phadnavis comes in, dancing a little. He holds a flower. All rise Nana gestures. Sit down, sit down. The music stops, Nana sits on a high seat. All are below him. Nana ogles the women, smells the flower, does not pay attention to the Kirtan. The sutradhar as Haridasa – sings an abhanga. Nana leers at the women. They are uneasy. Some adjust their saris. No noise now just gestures. The abhanga changes to a Lavani, a change from a religious song to a love ballad. Nana looks unblinkingly at a pretty girl. She is beautiful, shy, innocent Nana walks towards the girl. Nana steps towards her like a cat."

The power makes Nana egoistic and he boasts to the girl.

"All your dreams this Nana will fulfill.. no one in Poona today has the audacity to watch the great Nana phadnavis !

The innocent girl points to the idol of Ganpati and says
He will see.

And a lecherous, Michiavellian politician with, no moral scruples mockingly replies. That idol of holiness? That all holy Ganpati? The maker of Good? Look, he has two wives One on this side. One on that side. If you sit on our lap, he won't say anything!

It is this disregard of the established institutions, which, although as a result of his insatiable desire for sex, symbolizes the decadent human values of the modern society. The idol a substitute for an invisible god is worshipped by human beings and is believed to generate awe and fear among the wrongdoers and keeps men on the path of rectitude. But when man, out of selfishness, plays god himself, the cult of idol worship loses all its significance and becomes a device in the hands of the vested interests to perpetuate exploitation.

The girl tries to remind him that he is of his father's age and the answer of Nana is again of cunning lecherous politician. He says:

"Only in age. But our devotion is only to this graceful image... Don't lose any more time. Youth will not come again, the bloom will not last. My dear. You are like a daughter to us – someone else's."

Nana tries to chase her but she escapes like a frightened deer. Nana sends a servant to catch but he returns with failure and the servant promises Nana that he will chase her and bring before Nana tomorrow. Adulterous Nana craves for her and says :

Oh, can we? Can we find her? How beautifully formed! What a lovely figure ! Did you see? Erect! Young! Tender! Ah! Ho, ho!, We've seen so many, handled so many but none like that one."

He pleads before his servant to get the girl only on that night. Being arrogant, he wants to get the girl through his power and says :

"We tell you, if she is found, than this Nine court Nana will conquer Hindustan! What a bosom! Buds just blossoming...... we'll squeeze them like this!

This physical lust of Nana symbolizes the contemporary politicians who with the coming of power indulge in sexuality. Recently in Gujarat some politicians are exposed being involved in sex scandal and Newspaper reported that political power brings intoxication of "Wealth" "Woman" and "wine. In India, a candidate who wanders on cycle or buses, for the canvassing of the election returns home in luxurious car within five years. Even the parties look at the Muscle power and Money power while selecting the candidate. With the arrival of the power, the leaders are seen in the company of women and wine. Recently a BJP tribal MP was arrested at the international airport for alleged human trafficking. He tried to take a woman and a teenaged boy to Canada on the diplomatic passports of his wife and son. It is reported that katara smuggled several persons across to UK, Canada and Us in the past three years so, when in India, the politicians talk about women empowerment such incidents expose the double-standards of politicians. The irony is that even after the scandal they come out from the trial safely. Like.the M.P sex scandal of a reputed leader of political wing, created uproar in India but he comes out as "Mr. clean" after the trial.

The MP's like Laxman Bangaru, Dilipsinh Judev, are **allegedly** involved in treachery bribe and forgery. So many politicians keep two wives legally and declare openly that "they want new item daily" .Now a days a politician leaders' identity is that he must be adulterous, lecherous, treacherous, forger (briber) etc. instead of social worker and this sad scenario of contemporary Indian politics is represented nicely by Tendulkar while depicting Nana and his court.

Nana being a slave to passions, has transformed Pune into a playground for the pleasure seekers. Seeing Nana's craving for Gauri, Ghashiram hands his daughter over to Nana with a sense of success in trapping Nana through sex. Nana gets Gauri, but he wants to enjoy her daily. Following lines give us a glimpse of lecherous ruler who begs from his subordinate his daughter.

"Nana   :   Just one more time Ghashiram. Just one

more time, you bastard."

Ghashiram, reminds him of social criticism he has to face as a father at Pune and like a clever politician suggests a deal to Nana.

"Ghashiram :   Sir, there is a way people will not talk, my daughter will not be humiliated openly in Poona – if you make a clear arrangement.

Nana   :   How?

Ghashiram :   All right, sir to shut people's mouths, Make me the Kotwal of Poona.

Nana has no alternative but to accept Ghashiram's offer if he wants Gauri. This is the victory of Nana and not of Ghashiram. Ghashiram is decided. He thinks he will enjoy power and will save Gauri once he is declared Kotwal of Pune. But he has failed to recognize the game of the politician Nana. Nana in his soliloquy powers out his inner urge :

Nana   :   Go, Ghashya, old bastard. We made you, we made you

Kotwal Raise hall if you wish. But you don't know the ways of this Nana. This time, there are two bullets in this gun. With the first one, we'll fell your luscious daughter. But with the second one middle make city of Poona dance. Ghashya child, you're a foreigner. I have put you on poona's back. why? As a countercheck to all those conspirators. You'll not be able to join them. They'll never trust you even if you do. Because you're a stranger, you're an outsider. We just raised a dog at our door to the position of the Kotwali! We are our sole support.... What'll happen is that our misdeeds will be credited to your account. We do it. Our Kotwal pays for it. The opportunity comes in the shape of Ghashiram and the luscious peach is at hand to be devoured by Nana. Excellent! yes, Ghashya be Kotwal. This Nana blesses you.

So, here we find sexuality and the strategy of deputation go side by side. Ghashiram thinks that he has succeeded in his clever plan, but tragically, he does not foresee the future trap into which he is entering, Nana has double advantage in appointing Ghashiram as the Kotwal one sexual and second political. He can enjoy his daughter as well as use him to counter the Brahmins of Pune, **Samik Bandhopadhyay, in this context writes** : Nana needs Ghashiram and Ghashiram needs Nana, but in the shifting game of power, it is only a temporary adjustment that Nana exploits as long as necessary and can drop unceremoniously the moment it has served its purpose:

Like ceremony, both religious and secular, the deceptions of deputation constitutes yet another device of power. The real power uses the masks of deputation to mediate the exercise of power; to hide from the victims the real face of power, so that all resistance is effectively defected. Intermediate democratic institutions, or the paraphernalia of bureaucracy, too often regarded as repositories of at least executive power, are more often than not masks or meditations that veil the actual exercise of power and hide the perpetrator from the eyes of the victim. Even as Ghashiram fool that he is, thinks that the Kotwali will mean power in his hands, Nana knows " What'll happen is that our misdeeds will be credited to your account," Earlier, Tendulkar has shown religiosity and sexuality combining in the strategies of power. Now he shows sexuality and the strategy of deputation working hand in hand. Once again Tendulkar has his quip to drive it home.

Nana   : Bastard you've got me in a narrow pass.

Ghashiram   : Yes the narrow pass of my only daughter.

Tendulkar, in his social criticism, is more concerned with the mechanism of power operating within society than with the economic and political implications and sources of that power.

Tendulkar, in Ghashiram Kotwal observes the operations of religiosity, sexuality, and deputationist politics as devices of power. In Modern India the political leaders in order to get their aims fulfilled depute on the top position their so called nearones. As long as their aims are served, the officials enjoy the life with all its charms but as soon as the aims are fulfilled, the officials become useless and even danger to the political leaders so they do not hesitate even to eliminate them from life. The politicians are even worst than the underworld Dons. As depicted in the film "Vastav" the politician keeps relations with underworld man and indulges in so many antisocial activities but when they find them hindrance on their way to success, they eliminate them from the world. The tradition of "Use and Throw" has become synonymous with political leaders and Tendulkar tries to focus on this scenario through the plight of Ghashiram.

Ghashiram thinks that with the arrival of power and money, he would be able to find a suitable bridegroom for his daughter Gauri, and she would be released from the cunning Nana. But he is shocked to hear that Nana is getting married again. In the play it is announced by Sutradhar. Nana is getting married seventh time and his bride is just only 14 years old. Sutradhar says.

My Nana's wedding!

The bridge's a young one!

My nana's wedding!

A tender blossoming bride.

A slender willowy bride

A slay lily – white bridge.

A just – this – year ripened bridge

My Nana's wedding!

The satire on the ruler of Pune is futher presented through one more song of Sutradhar.

Let's go to the wedding

The Peshwa's chief minister

Still young enough to marry!

His moustache's turned grey

Not all of them are gone

He's got six wives

Look – that's not enough!

So he's got a new one.

She needs a companion

So-

Lusty Nana indulges in the tradition of polygamy and keeps on getting married as soon as he is fed up with the newly-wedded wife. Generally the ruler of the country follows the moral code of conduct in life so his life style inspires the country men and he sets the example of morality before the citizens. But here power brings adultery in Nana and he neglects the social rules, regulations and restrains. He becomes the transgresser. This very behaviour of Nana reflects the behaviour of contemporary politicians, who illegally keep two wives and extra-marital relations. Power and money become instrument for such leaders to satisfy their physical lust. It becomes easy for them to get a girl with the help of power and money and the exploitation of the girl continues. Tendulkar through another song sarcastically presents this reality:

(All together)

The groom comes over the threshold. How did the groom get his bride? He gave three hundred gold coins. And so he bought the bride. My Nana's wedding.

The groom has come near the altar. How did the groom get his bride? He gave a great big gift of land, That's how he bought his bride.

Instead of using the money of the state on the welfare of society the ruler satisfies his personal motives. A woman remains a commodity to buy and purchase and the ruler like Nana enjoys life with the help of power and money. Ghashiram, hearing about Nana's marriage, rushes to his palace and makes an inquiry about his daughter Gauri. Nana ignores him and gives random answers regarding Gauri. But when he finds rage in Ghashiram's eyes, he says: Nana! Yes, I'll tell you. She….. she….. she…. To Chandra the midwife!

The newly-wedded wife of Nana is horrified by Ghashirams anger and Nana pacifies his wife by saying

Nana   : Are you afraid, dear? We could finish him, off

with just a gesture of this hand. Come on.. Let's go.

Nana is confident that being ruler no one can question him and Ghashiram is merely his servant. And the time to throw Ghashiram from his ruling system has arrived. His purpose is solved. His daughter Gauri he has enjoyed and now he is no more interested in withered flower like Gauri. Ghashiram comes to know that his daughter died as she was pregnant and buried too. Nana has used her and thrown her too from his life. For the untimely death of Gauri Nana is responsible. Ghashiram can not control himself and accuses Nana for the pre-mature death of Gauri.

He says

Ghashriam   : You deceive me, Nanasahib. You did this you

took my child's life. My only child. My innocent darling…. You killed…… Nana is also surprised to see that his deputy is speaking and accusing him for the murder openly so with anger he says –

Nana   : Are you mad you fool ! Ghashya child. These

hands have never killed even an insect… In these hands is only the flute of Lord Krishna which made the Gopis forget hunger and thirst. And you should think before you accuse the Peshwa's Chief minister. Are you thinking clearly, Ghashya ? To Whom do you speak with such subordination? The Peshwa's Chief minister stands before you, Ghashya –

Nana even tries to pacify Ghashiram by giving the philosophy of life and death and even instructs him to perform his duty of Kotwali well and he should forget his grief. He is so cunning and crocodile-skinned man that he reminds him that he should not talk about Gauri's death as not Nana but people will criticize Ghashiram for having sold his daughter so it would bring disgrace to Ghashiram only and not to Nana. He advises Ghashiram not to mention the incident of Gauri's death in the society as it will defame Gauri only, and he also suggests that if Ghashiram hears only gossip regarding Gauri's death and Nana, he should punish the gossiper severly. This behaviour of Nana symbolizes the approach of the contemporary hard-hearted politicians who are self-oriented and pleasure-seekers. The word "Death" does not move them. On the contrary, they plan out strategy to remain out of the scandal, though they themselves are the centre of the scandal. As soon as Ghashiram departs, Nana orders servant –

Nana   : Remove Gauri's corpse and throw it in the river. If anyone finds so much as a bone, I'll break your bones......

And goes away to enjoy his newly-wedded wife. Politician or leader and their lust for physical body is universal and age-old issue. Sex scandals are often associated with movie stars, politicians or others in the public eye and become scandals largely because of the prominence of the person involved. The contemporary politicians like Nana too enjoy extra-marital relations or sex and use their political power to satisfy it. This is universal occurence. Let's take a glance of the politicians or leaders of the world.

1. David Blankett : Resigned as UK Home secretary after it was revealed he had an affair with a married woman kimberley quinn and was alleged to have used his position to speed up a visa application by her Nanny.

2. **John & Brownlee, a former primier of Alberta** was forced to resign in 1934 after allegations that he seduced a young woman.

3. **Chu Mei- feng, a former Taiwanese female politician**, could only cut off all relationships with Taiwan after a local magazine published a video CD showing her having sex with married businessman Tseng Chung- ming in 2001.

4. **Eduina eurrie** revealed in 2002 that she had a four year extra marital affair with John Major who would later become prime Minister,

5. Lord, Lamblon, a minister in the UK Government of Edward Heath, was forced to resign in disgrace in 1973 after it was revealed that he had used prostitute and marijuana.

6. Former US Representative Bob Linvingston resigned as a speaker of the United State House of Representatives and the US congress in December 1998 after it was revealed during the height of the impeachment debate surrounding the Lewinsky scandal

7. The Lewinsky scandal, in which sitting **American president Bill Clinton** engaged in a variety of sexual activity with his intern Monica Lewinsky. Clinton's denial under oath made it worse and created, apart from the embarrassment, a legal problem that led to his trial for impeachment, for which he was acquitted, serving the rest of his term duly.

8. In **India r**ecently Two senior politicians of India-administered **Kashmir Ghulam Ahmed Mir** and **Raman Matto** were arrested in connection with a sex scandal involving an underage girl. The affair has led to widespread protest in Kashmir. Both politicians were state ministers in the Kashmir coalition Government. The accused are alleged to have misused their authority to force underage girl into prostitution in Kashmir.

Nana savours Gauri's innocent charm as long as his sensuality is satisfied and turns to another woman. Ghashiram is shocked and becomes more ruthless and brutal. He locks up the Brahmins for stealing fruits and they die due to suffocation in the jail. 22 are dead and this incident makes the Poonite Brahmins to raise voice against Ghashiram. They demand for Ghashiram's death and Nana signs the death warrant as casually, as he had granted Ghashiram the Kotwali, Sutradhar says –

Brahmans! Ho! Listen! Listen! As per your demands, the Peshwa's chief minister Nana Phadnavis has given the order for Ghashiram Kotwal's execution. First shave his head and anoint it with sinder. Then run him around town on a camel. Tie him to an elephant's leg and lastly give him the sentence of death. At the very end, tie one of his hands behind his back and let Ghashiram Savaldas face the mob.

Nana wins the game as he is cleverer and he gets the opportunity to remove Ghashiram from his court as now he is useless and danger to him. He says :

Nana : Use a thorn to take out a thorn. That's great. The disease has been stopped. Anyway, he was no use any more.

The final scene shows Ghashiram being mobbed by the irate crowd and he is stoned to death. As the crowd gathers round Ghashiram's lifeless body. Nana appears to herald the end of an age of terror and prosper festivity to make the purging of the city. Nana says

Nana : Ladies and gentlemen. Citizens of Poona. A threat to the great city of Poona has been ended today. A disease has been controlled. The demon Ghashya kotwal who plagued all of us, has met his death. Everything has happened according to the wishes of the gods. The mercy of the gods is with us always.

Let the corpse of sinful Ghashya rot. Let the wolves and dogs have it. Let the worms have it., whoever attempts to take away this corpse will be punished, whoever mourns for him, will be hanged. And living relatives of Ghashya salvaldas will be found bound and expelled from the city. We have ordered that from this day forward, not a word, not a stone relating to the sinner shall survive. We have commanded that there be festivities for three days to mark this happy occasion.

Thus, the story of Nana and Ghashiram shows politics as a game of power and also the evils related with power politics, the play has attracted a large number of spectators the world over. **N.S Dharan** avers in the following words.

"The inescapable reality is that as long as politics remains a power game phadnavis, Ghashirams, and Lalita Gauris are bound to emerge. Not only in India but also the worldover. We witness, Ghashiram kotwals being played on real political theatres. This universal political reality in fact accounts for the abiding popularity of the play".

The statement is absolutely correct. Nana and the plight of Ghashiram refer to the present day, game of politics, recently in Gujarat the three IPS – Officers - DIG D.G. Vanzara, superintendent of Police Rajkumar Pandian and Rajasthan SP Dinesh MN were arrested (The kotwals) in connection with the fake encounter of Sohrabudin sheikh (22,23,2005 Nov.) The probe revealed that his wife Kauserbi was murdered a few days after her hushand was killed.

The three police officers are suspended and the State Government has not taken any action to save them, though the encounter (Fake) must be done with the permission of the Chief

Minister. Once again this recent incident of Gujarat shows the "use and throw "principle of the ruler and this very sad reality is presented by Tendulkar through the story of Nana and Ghashiram.

4. METAMORPHOSIS OF GHASHIRAM:- FROM DOCILE FATHER TO A CUNNING FATHER.

Vijay Tendulkar's dramatic creation reflects his concern for common man who, caught in the matrix of opportunistic ethics of modern world feels alienated. Ghashiram Kotwal shows how a common-man hero, seeking power, confronts the people who are already in power and undergoes an organic change.

Ghashiram Kotwal, though based on historical legend, is not actually a historical play. It is more concerned with the life of Ghashiram, the common-man hero than with the history of Nana Phadnavis. It tells the story of a person who, confronted with a world of hypocrisy and inhumanity, learns to play a careerist falling in line with prevailing ethics and becomes a martyr. The play gains in metaphoric dimension as the central character's obsession with power results in the loss of his identity.

Ghashiram's transformation from an ordinary person to the tyrannical executor of power and to an ordinary person again is more eventful than the story of Nana Phadanavis. It is the story of the rise from anonymity of Ghashiram Savaldas to the kotwalship of Poona, and his inevitable fall and gruesome end.

According to history, Ghashiram was a North Indian Brahmin, a resident of Aurangabad, who was appointed as the police prefect of Poona on 8th Feb, 1777 and continued to hold office till his death which took place on 31st August 1791 under violent circumstances. He had earned Nana's confidence by his faithful service during the critical times that followed the Peshwa Narayan Rao's murder. He enjoyed the full trust of Nana Phadnavis and his administration was notoriously worse than that of his predecessors. He was the man who had been appointed to watch the movements and plans of Raghunath Rao and his family and he reported to Nana whatever suited his purpose. He had under him a large body of unscrupulous spies, everyone possessing ample means of harassing innocent people and as a consequence the word 'Ghashiram' has become a permanent synonym for oppression and tyranny.

Tendulkar has used this piece of history for the play to show the metamorphosis of Ghashiram. Ghashiram, the protagonist is a poor Brahmin from Kannauj who comes to Pune in search of a livelihood. Pune is dominated by local Brahmins who distinguished themselves as scholars, doctors, logicians, astrologers, linguisst and barons. While Ghashiram has no identity and patronage, so he has no high hopes for life. What worries him is how to earn a living for his family in the caste society of Pune. We meet him at bavannakhani, a red light district at Pune, where Gulabi, a courtesan entertains Nana, and his followers with dance and song. Ghashiram takes refuge at there in order to feed his family.

It is here Ghashiram gets the chance to meet Nana who appears to him as his saviour but he does not know his destiny that his saviour will be his destructer. The city is rotten as the ruler Nana, with lack of morality, married seven times, and is still running after young women. At Bavannkhani on the name of God, a dance of adultery is going on and the Brahmins and Nana are enjoying Gulabi's dance and join her in dance. During the dance Nana hurts his ankle and Ghashiram saves him by offering his back to rest his injured leg. Ghashiram who has struggled a lot to establish himself in the society takes up a chance to please Nana. The resourcefulness of Ghashiram pleases Nana and he offers necklace to Ghashiram for saving him. But this reward from Nana to Ghashiram instills wrath and jealousy in Brahmins.

When Nana is pleased with Ghashiram, Gulabi introduces him thus Gulabi "He came four days ago. He dances with me. He was a foreigner, going without food. I said, let him stay here. He washes my utensils. Sings for me. Does all sorts of thing."

It suggests that Ghashiram is ready to do any work, at any house to maintain his existence. Though born Brahmin, he is ready to do any low work. Nana gives him necklace. Gulabi, tries to snatch away necklace from Ghashiram. She reminds him that she has given him shelter and hired him as a servant so he was able to meet Nana and legally the necklace should be given to Gulabi. But Ghashiram, who is struggling hard to survive, is unwilling to part with the necklace as it would be his means of livelihood and he will not have to work at such a degraded place like Bavannakhani. So he cries "It's mine, it's mine." But the servants for Gulabi snatch away the necklace and throw him out. This is the first humiliation Ghashiram faces at Pune.

This scene leads to the scene of Dakshina ceremony. Tendulkar portrays excellently the pathetic condition of the Brahmins. Nana makes a mockery of this sacred ceremony using it as a device to achieve his selfish ends. He feels happy as the Brahmins in their eagerness to grub the gifts fight like dogs. When Ghashiram tries to join them for alms, they throw him out. They hand him over to the soldiers, blaming him for the theft of a purse. Inspite of his innocence, he is punished severely and locked up in a cell. He continues to cry that he is not a theif but in vain. The sutradhar, in the role of fellow prisoner tries to console him and advises him to sleep and to take rest. Ghashiram is still unable to understand what crime he had committed. He says

But I didn't steal. I swear to God I didn't. I'm not a thief. I'm from Kanauj. I'm a Brahman. I've been here two weeks. I came here to find my fortune – and lost my reputation. How did it happen? What will happen to my wife? To my daughter? What will they say when they hear of this?

His self-respect is injured. He feels as if the days of honesty, morality, values, respect are gone. The world is ruled by the evil force and one has to merge into evil in order to sustain oneself. He wants to lead a civilized life with his family. He comes at Pune as an innocent person, a man who loves his family dearly. He hopes that the city of Pune will provide him better means of livelihood with which he would make the life of his daughter happy. But this innocent imagination of Ghashiram is crushed when he is labeled as "Thief". His poverty becomes hindrance in the way of success. Even the people are not ready to consider him as Brahmin. They laugh at his non-Brahmin look and say –

> You a Brahmin!
> Where is your shaven head?
> Where is your holy thread?
> Where is your pious look?
> Where is your holy book?
> Recite the hierarchy of caste!
> Tell us, when did you last fast?

So, Tendulkar here satires that the world is going by deceptive looks. Being poor Ghashiram can not represent himself as a traditional Brahmin. But from within he is pure, possessing the qualities of hard work, honesty, love, commitment but the world is unable to justify him even as a man. The theme of Appearance V\s Reality is clearly brought out. From the outward appearance Ghashiram is banished from the folk of Brahmins but in reality from within he is pious Brahmin. Whereas the punites Brahmins outwardly appear pious but actually they, do not deserve the title of Brahmin if we examine their deeds. They indulge, in adultery and get pleasure in the company of other women. They are hypocrites as they hide their misdeeds under the name of religion. They regard

Bavannakhani the red-light area, as "Mathura Avatarli" associated with Lord Krishna. It shows their disrespect for the religious institutions. Yet the society regard them as pious Brahmins and Ghashiram who is genuine is considered as non-brahmin and thief. The theme of appearance v\s reality is further explored when the suthradhar says –

> "The thief is a simple thief
> The police are official thieves.
> If a thief wants to live
> To the police he's got to give.
>
> You need protection money.
> And on top of that
> Their mercy might end any time
> And so will you."

Again it is revealed that the protectors of the city are too deceptive. They wear Khakhi, the disguise of the protection, but in reality they are the biggest enemies of the citizens. Under their mercy crimes are hidden or explored.

In a world where hatred, jealously and immorality are the order of the day, even the most innocent people like Ghashiram are bound to be affected. Ghashiram's confrontation with the soldiers and his humiliation precipitate his innermost protest against injustice and inhumanity. Being motivated by a powerful vindictive desire, he swears to teach a lesson to the perpetrators of crime.

The soldiers release him from the cell and throw him out by saying –

"Get lost, Hey! Thief, monkey. If you so much as put a foot in the holy city of Poona, you'll lose your head. Go away. Take your ugly face far away. Don't come back to Poona. Not even your shadow fall on the city of Poona. Get lost. Go."

This cruelity forces him to take a vow to avenge his humiliation.

He says –

"But I'll come back. I'll come back to Poona. I'll show my strength. It will cost you! Your good days are gone! I am a kanauj Brahman. But I've become a shudra, a criminal, a useless animal. There is no one to stop me now, to mock me, to make me bend, to cheat me. Now I am a devil. You've made me an animal. I'll be a devil inside. I'll come back like a boar and I'll stay as a devil. I'll make pigs of all of you. I'll make this Poona a kingdom of pigs. Then I'll be Ghashiram again, the son of Savaldas once more."

It is a turning point in the play and the play changes into a revenge play Ashok kumar Sharma in his article "Ghashiram kotwal: A study in the politics of power and Revenge." Writes

"Generally the reason for revenge is hurting of one's self respect or honour or loss of love or betrayal. Draupadi's taking oath in Mahabharat or Chanakya's taking oath to destroy the ruler of Magadh may be compared with Ghashiram Savaldas' oath. "Ghashiram kotwal" may be compared with "Spanish Tragedy." "Hamlet" and "Duchess of Malfi."

The repeated humiliation of Ghashiram forces him to enter into the world of corruption in order to conquer the evil forces. He was not ambitious person or raves for power and money. He is a common man but his every effort to keep his family up leads him to realization that in a world where humanity is at a discount it is hard to assert his individuality. So he searches out a way. He comes to know about the weakness of Nana – that he is a womanizer and can do anything for the sheer company of a woman. So he decides to use his own daughter Lalita Gauri as a bait court. Now the seed of power is sown in his mind and for that he is ready to go to any extent.

Ghashiram's craving for power may be compared with Dr. Faustes' craving of power. In order to conquer the world, just as Dr. Faustus sells his soul to the devil Mephistophilis , here also Ghashiram sells his soul – his own daughter Gauri to enjoy the power. In a religious ceremony Nana sees Gauri and is fascinated by her. He tries to chase her but in vain. He becomes mad for her and Ghashiram decides to sacrifice her with a hope that with the arrival of power he will release her from the clutches of Nana. Smita Mishra in her article "Ghashiram kotwal as a political play" writes –

"Seeing Nana's craving for Gauri, Ghashiram hands his daughter over to Nana with a sense of success in trapping Nana through sex. For a moment he is torn by a conflict between an individual motivated by a sense of revenge and a responsible father. He feels the prick of conscience and cries out "…….. oh my daughter ….. the beast! Oh, you people. Look! I've given my beloved daughter into the jaws of that wolf! Look, look at this father. Putting the child of his heart up for sale. Look at my innocent daughter – a whore. That old overripe bastard! Look at him, eating her like a peach…. Spit on me. Stone me. Look, look but I will not quit. I'll make this Poona a kingdom of pigs." So Ghashiram is left with no other alternative than to sacrifice his daughter to realize his dream. Dream of turning the city of Pune into a kingdom of pigs and wielding unquestionable power. He exploits Nana's sexual weakness to his advantage. Thus we find in Ghashiram a metamorphosis from a docile father to a cunning schemer."

He knows that Nana wants Gauri by any means, so instead of protecting her or going away from Poona in order to save her from the clutches of Nana, Ghashiram like a clever politician, in order to get power, makes a deal with Nana. He commits himself a terrible sin by prostituting his own daughter. He first reminds Nana about his helplessness, the social criticism that he will have to bear for becoming the panderer of his own daughter. In order to avoid such circumstances he himself suggests a remedy and says

Ghashiram   : All right sir, to shut people's mouths, make me
               the Kotwal of Poona.

And Nana has no choice but to surrender to the will of Ghashiram. So, Ghashiram who wants to drive sin out of Pune, surrenders his "heart's child" to Nana for mere kotwalship. Ghashiram feels that he has succeeded in his clever plan, but tragically he does not foresee the future trap into which he is entering. Nana has double advantage in appointing Ghashiram as the Kotwal: Fulfillment of carnal desire and political necessity.

Ghashiram takes on the duty of looking after Pune. He does his work sincerely. He enforces the laws strictly and declares that the trangressors shall be punished severely. As a result there is an enormous fall in the crime rate. Sutradhar says – Ghashiram gave an order

1) No whoring without a permit.

2) No cremation without a permit.

3) Ghashiram Kotwal says to eat with a lower caste person is a crime.

Scared by his method of punishment the Brahmins shudder at the mention of is name. He announces nothing can be done without his notice. Permits should be obtained. Sutradhar says –

"Ghashiram kotwal says to kill a pig, to do an abortion, to be a pimp, to commit a misdemeanour, to steal, to live with one's divorced wife, to remarry if one's husband is alive, to hide one's caste, to use counterfeit coins, to commit suicide, without a permit is a sin. A good man may not prostitute himself, a Brahman may not sin, without a permit."

Sutradhar further says –

"Ghashiram Kotwal started making the rounds of Poona at night, after the eleven o'clock cannon. Started ruling in person, Accosted anyone he met in the streets. Whipped people. Arrested people. Demanded people's permits. Imprisoned people. Sued people."

So, Ghashiram is able to bring order in the city. And Tendulkar wants to suggest that order, Ram-Rajaya is possible if the leader is transparent and committed to his duty. People are ready to obey the orders. But if the leader himself is interested in immorality, anarchy may arise in the state. Here sutradhar informs the audience that crimes are lessened. As the prisons start filling. The Brahmins have to stay at night with their wives instead of Bavannakhani. Even the wives have to sleep with the men they are married. The heart of Poona is Bavannakhani but now it has lost its heart. Sutradhar says

"They are compelled to be moral not to abort, to be wholesome, to stay alive.

He further says –

"Prostitutes' Lane was desolate. The chasing of women was halted. Pimps turned into beggars. Counterfeit coins were worthless. Sin was worthless.

Ghashiram's character can be analysed from the psycho-analysis point also. He is deeply hurt by his humiliation so that humiliation has left an indelible mark on his subconscious mind. So though he gets power and brings order in the city his subconscious mind always reminds him that the city is not orderly and whoring is continued at night. This illusion makes him suspicious and violent. Whosoever he meets at night whether a man or woman, he thinks he/she is involved in prostitution. So unnecessarily he punishes them and brings (disrespect) harm to his own image as Kotwal. Smita Mishra writes

"Surprisingly, Ghashiram blinded by his success, turns demoniac. His imposition of rules on the behaviour of the people reaches the height of absurdity. He misuses his power. For a moment, the city of Pune seems to get rid of its vulgarity under the strict vigilance of Ghashiram Kotwal. But there is a rise in evil activities too. The effect of absolute power on Ghashiram makes him ruthless, sadist and highhanded in his treatment of the people who have hurt his feelings earlier. He employs savage techniques to elicit truth from culprits. No doubt, the kotwalship serves as a means to bring about a change in the city but soon he becomes impatient and fails to understand the real cause for the crimes of the people. In no time, he becomes unpopular."

Let us see, few examples, how he brings unpopularity for himself by punishing and harassing the innocent needy people.

Ghashiram   : idiot! It's a good thing I caught you. Where are

You going?

Sutradhar	: Nowhere, my lord.
Ghashiram	: To steal?
Sutradhar	: No, sir.
Ghashiram	: To whore?
Sutradhar	: No, no sir.
Ghashiram	: Tell the truth.
Sutradhar	: No, no sir.
Ghashiram	: Then where?
Sutradhar	: Home.
Ghashiram	: Whose home? Tell the truth which whore were you going to?
Sutradhar	: No, sir, to my own house.
Ghashiram	: Then why are you out this late? Speak quickly.
Sutradhar	: Sir, I was going to fetch the midwife.
Ghashiram	: Midwife. Who's delivering?
Sutradhar	: My wife.
Ghashiram	: Why does she deliver in the middle of the night. Speak up.
Sutradhar	: Her time had come!
Ghashiram	: Where is the midwife?
Sutradhar	: She wouldn't come. Said she didn't have a permit. Said she'd come after the four o'clock cannon.
Ghashiram	: Good. Have you got a permit? Speak.
Sutradhar	: No, sir.
Ghashiram	: Why not? Go out on the road at night without a permit and you will get whipped.

Sutradhar : Have pity, sir.

Ghashiram : (hits him) Why didn't you get a permit?

Sutradhar : I didn't know she was going to deliver at night.

Ghashiram : what ! you didn't know when your wife would deliver? She's your wife isn't she?

Sutradhar : Yes, sir, don't hit me.

Ghashiram : (to a soldier) Go with him. Go to his house and make sure if his lying, take off his shirt and give him twenty-five lashes. If he is a thief, an adulterer, a whore-monger, then he up his hands and feet and throw him in a cell.

Ghashiram : I'll straighten out this adulterous city in six months!

In another incident one woman complains –

Sir, listen to my complaint. My husband and his brothers have been arrested by the kotwal's soldiers. My father – in – law died. They wont' let them hold the funeral. The permit is real, but they call it counterfeit. Sir- the corpse has been lying in the cremation ground since morning. The dogs are gathering. Sir-please-give us justice.

But Ghashiram is stubborn. He has gone mad in his mission of bringing order n the city. His sensibilities and emotions are dead. He says –

If anyone is seen throwing powder at anyone but his wife, bind his hands. Morality must be protected. Take away the Brahmans who are having too good a time! Just a little fun without any vulgarity is all right. Keep a sharp ear out. Keep a sharp eye out. Demand permit."

Once he catches one Brahman and changes him as a thief, though he is innocent. He is not ready to accept that he is a thief. And he is severly punished. Sutradhar says –

"The soldiers come! The nails of the Brahman's right hand are pulled out. The fingers are washed with lemon juice and soap. All the lines and signs of his hand are noted. His hands are wrapped in a bag and the bag is sealed.

Ghashiram derives sadistic pleasure while seeing the Brahman being punished. The Brahman begs for mercy. But Ghashiram says –

"The ordeal shall be done. The ordeal shall be done. You heretic! Bring that hot ball over here. Hold his hands, tightly. If he yells, don't let go. Let his hands burn. You should smell them burning. Smell them!"

The Brahman curses him and says

"I did not steal. I did not steal. I did not steal. O, Ghashiram, you have tormented a poor innocent Brahman. You'll die without children! You yourself will die. Will endure torment greater than mine. You'll die a dog's death, grinding your heels in the dirt. So Ghashiram has been digging his grave inch-by-inch following the path of callousness and vindictiveness. The moral law, which he has been violating, will one day assert itself and crush him. His crimes border on sins and will be balanced by retribution. Being ignorant of all this he continues with his work which adds to the dramatic irony. But then in the course of these things, though he appears to be carried away by absolute power, he is aware of his responsibility as a father. He says –

I've got the kotwali and I've got Poona straightened out! All these hard, proud Brahmans are soft as cotton now. No one dares to look Ghashiram straight in the eye! Now, once I find a fitting husband for my darling daughter – that piece of my heart named Lalita Gauri and get her married, then everything will be the way I want it. I'll make such a show of the wedding that no one's tongue will dare utter one bad word about my daughter. And if some tongue starts wagging, it's easy to cut it off! Nowfirst- I'll look! Now-first- I'll look for a bridegroom when one has money, jewels, and respect! And my daughter's beautiful – one in a million! I'll send my men out right now to look for a husband, and I'll arrange everything."

But his dream is shattered. He comes to know about his daughter's death and Nana's another wedding. She was preganant and so Nana was no more interested in her. He realizes the cunning plan of Nana and he bursts out on the grave of Gauri –

Oh, my child, My Gauri. A piece of my heart. Oh! Oh! Oh! Oh! What has become of you! What happened? What did that devil Nana do? That monster."

He blames Nana but Nana tries to pacifiy him. Ghashiram buries the grief of his daughter's death in his heart silently as he finds himself the culprit for the death. He realises that he has got power and fame, but has lost he priceless gift of God. For the tragic death of his daughter he cannot blame Nana solely, as he willingly handed over his daughter to him for the sheer pleasure of power. He knew Nana and his scheme yet he sacrificed his daughter. Now it appears useless to him. The power with which he wanted to enhance the happiness of his daughter has made him impotent. Such a shock transforms Ghashiram into a fiend who suddenly shuts his eyes to immorality and plunges headlong into a career of bloodshed. The death of his daughter made him insensitive as well as revengeful.

Sutradhar says –

1) The way a wounded tiger becomes addicted to blood, so the Kotwal has come to love the smell.

Others : The Kotwal has acquired a penchant for human blood.

Sutradhar : The Kotwal for the slightest reason beats and kills in any season.

The mouths of Poona people were dry with fear.

Others : Dry with fear.

Sutradhar : No one's life was guaranteed. Fear cut life in half, Indeed!

Once a group of foreign Brahmans arrive at Poona at night. Since they are hungry, they eat mangoes form the garden without asking and Ghashiram arrests them on the charge of stealing fruits. He orders to lock them all in the cell for the night. But the cell was very small to accommodate one group. Sutradhar says –

The Brahmans in the cell can't get enough air. They are suffocating. They are moaning. They are in torment. They're calling for help. But who will help? Everyone's asleep. The guards are high on opium. During the night, some of the Brahmans died."

Twenty-two are dead, and the rest are half-dead. The sardar who is an enemy of Ghashiram gets a golden chance. He makes a complaint to the Peshwa. He pleads that a penalty of death for stealing fruit is too much and the Peshwa becomes furious and meets Nana. The Brahmins also gather against Nana's house and demand justice as they want to put an end on the cruelty of Ghashiram's reign, and Nana who has already enjoyed his daughter finds Ghashiram useless. His purpose is solved and he passes the order of sentence of death for Ghashiram.

Nana : Oh shit, is that all? Bring my pen, you idiot. Bring paper. Take this. Take it. Give it to them. The order for Ghashya's death. Give it to e'm. tell them to be happy. Tell them to humiliate him all they want."

The irate crowd stoned him to death as sutradhar says –

They shaved his head.

They sindur-daubed his head.

They road him around on a camel.

They tied him to the leg of an elephant.

The city of Poona watched it all.

Injured Ghashiram while dying says –

Ghashiram Savaldas! Ghashiram Savaldas! I danced on your chests but I wasted the life of my little daughter. I should be punished for the death of my daughter. Beat me. Beat me. Hit me. Cut off my hands and feet. Crack my skull. Come on. Look! I'm here. Oh, that's good. Very good. **Smita Mishra** in her article **"Ghashiram Kotwal as a political play"** writes

"Ghashiram is outwitted at the game of power played by Nana who exploits him as long as he needs him and drops him brutally in the end. Ghashiram's transformation from a poor and helpless Brahmin to a highhanded Kotwal is a journey from the world of innocence to the world of experience.

The title of the play itself captivates its essence. It unites the public and the private being of a man. It is the transformation of a simple, unassuming man into a hubristic power crazy monster. The unsuspecting victim of a Machiavellian system embodied in the machinations of Nana. The true villain emerges unseathed from the turmoil that marked the rise and fall of Ghashiram.

The punishment meted out to Ghashiram proves the formula that who negates the universal order gets negated by it ultimately.

Ghashiram rightly deserves our pity for the punishment is greater than he deserved. There is a tragic sense of waste illustrated by the death of Ghashiram. Tendulkar has presented a very striking picture of a tragic figure like Ghashiram. Ghashiram Savaldas belongs not only to the late eighteenth century Peshwa Empire, but also to all phases of human history. His rise and growth from a Savaldas to the most controversial Kotwal of Pune is symbolic of the multifaceted growth of corruption in our society. Through the shrewd and opportunistic character of Ghashiram, Tendulkar has tried to bring out the truth that sycophancy not only flourishes but also prospers under the patronage of the rulers. Ghashiram knowingly puts his daughter at the disposal of a wolf like Nana so as to satisfy his ambition. As a Kotwal he gets complete hold over the city of Pune and behaves with the people in a ruthless manner. He gives physical as well as mental torture to the common, innocent people. His cruelty crosses all the limits of reasonable human behaviour. Ghashiram is stoned to death on account of his indiscriminately revengeful spirit. He chooses evil deliberately, sticks to it and finally pays for it.

In depicting the rise and growth of Ghashiram in our society, Tendulkar seems to have suggested that the purpose of the drama is not to produce catharsis i.e. "Peace of mind; all passion spent" but to encourage, stimulate and provoke the audience\reader to think over the issues affecting the normal and balanced growth of human society. By showing the fatal end of Ghashiram in the play, Tendulkar does not want to suggest that Ghashiram has ended forever. He rather wants to draw our attention to the socio-political factors responsible for the growth of such a crisis in our society. There are certain questions that keep haunting our minds. What led to the emergence of Ghashiram? Who is responsible for the rise and growth of Ghashiram? And what are the fatal consequences arising out of the creation of Ghashiram? The contemporary relevance of the play lies in the answer to these questions, and here Tendulkar stands firmly as a class by himself."

R.N. Rai writes in **"Ghashiram Kotwal A Search for Socio-individual crisis"**

"Ghashiram's character may be compared to the character of Shakespeare's Macbeth. Just as Macbeth meets his fatal end on account of the flaw of over ambitiousness, Ghashiram is stoned to death on account of his indiscriminately revengeful spirit. Ghashiram would have got the stature of an Aristotelian tragic hero if Tendulkar had introduced soliloquies in order to reveal the real good character of Ghashiram who had come to Poona in order to earn his livelihood. But as the play stands, we realize that Ghashiram chooses evil deliberately sticks to it and ultimately pays for it. There are numerous scenes of suffering in the play which are capable of arousing pity and fear......."

Even the same opinion is given by **Basava raj Nalkar** in **"Ghashiram Kotwal : A Tragedy of Power"**.

"Ghashiram easily brings to our mind Macbeth who continues to follow the wrong path even after losing lady Macbeth. He was so much intoxicated with his power and ambition that he could not leave in the middle of the course. In a similar manner, Ghashiram, far from resigning from the post of Kotwal, continues in the same position to take further revenge upon the citizens of Pune…

5. THE WORLD OF WOMEN IN PESHWA'S EMPIRE

"Women have been called queens for a long time, but the kingdom given them isn't worth ruling."

Since time immemorial women are considered as a secondary sex. She is exploited in one way or the other way. And if we look at this play from the feministic point of view the play presents suppressed lot of women. Tendulkar always tries to present the feminine world in a patriarchal society. In his major plays he tries to explore the world and psyche of women. He believes that whether a woman is educated or not, the social structure and conventions never allow her freedom or space she lives under the patriarchal authority, - submissive and suppressed. He presents the female characters not as subsidary caste or only as show-piece on the stage but much more emphasis is given to them. For example **Leela Benare** in *Silence! The court is in session*

Sarita and Kamala in *Kamala* **Manik and Rama** in *Vulture* **Laxmi and Champa** in *Sakharam Binder*, **Jyoti** in *Kanyadaan* and **Lalita Gauri** in *Ghashiram Kotwal*. As **Smita Mishra** writes.

"On looking at the play also from a feministic point of view, it presents a very moving, even shocking picture of the ruthless suppression of feminine consciousness. Tendulkar shows how vulnerable Indian Women are in our patriarchal society. Ghashiram, the eponymous father, does not hesitate in bargaining the chastity of his daughter for his own selfish desire to avenge his humiliation on the people of Pune. For Nana Phadnavis woman is an object of sexual gratification only. Nana procures Gauri by making Ghashiram the Kotwal of Pune and for sometime as is reported by the sutradhar:

"Ghashiram says, Nana does, Ghashiram reign is here.

Nana however has such an endless lust for women that he always needs a beautiful girl and a new bride for the gratification of his sexual urges. Gauri's physical charms cannot satisfy him for long and it is soon reported that Nana is marrying a girl of fourteen. Marriage is considered to be the holiest of holy institutions in our society. But Nana has a different way of looking at the sanctity of marriage. Inspite of having several wives he's still going to marry a small girl.

Woman has no choice of her own in a male dominated society and the situation is the same whether she is Gulabi or Gauri or the newlywed wife of Nana or the old wives of Nana. Woman has always been a slave to her male counterpart, be it the eighteenth century or the twenty – first century.

In words of **Gayle Greene** and **Coppelia Kalin** :

"Women are the gifts which men exchange between each other….. they are gifts not givers they have no significant power or influence within a system. Which is controlled by men and world to their benefit. Men, not women, have the power to determine the values of women in the exchange and the meanings associated with them."

Tendulkar throughout the play has used female sexuality to represent the loss and destruction caused by the struggle for power. The corruption that power brings about is projected through the sexual laxity of the Brahmin dominated society of Pune. The play was attacked by those who perceived the play as an attack on the character of Nana Phadnavis, the finest administrator and one of the greatest patriots of the Maratha Empire. Tendulkar responded to this criticism by pointing out that Ghashiram Kotwal was not meant to be a historically accurate account of Nana or Ghashiram's character or the rule over Pune. The most important thing is that he has examined the very modern issue of the relationship between power and gender in a patriarchal society in a historical setting with historically recognizable characters. Tendulkar has underlined both

the dark ambiguity of the cardboard figures of power which the male dominated society holds in high esteem and the dangers of this struggle for power in which gender has always played an important part. Meaning of gender in patriarchy is not just "difference" but division, oppression, inequity and inferiority for women." And thus for all those without access to power. Tendulkar in Ghashiram Kotwal suggests that the social construction of gender is effectively a useful tool in the hands of the powerful and will lead inevitably to the dehumanizing of both the powerful and the powerless alike, the Nanas and the Ghashirams as much as the Gauris, and also brought the destruction of meaningful human relationships and social and moral values."

Tendulkar again in this play shows woman's exploitation in a male dominated society through the depiction of Lalita Gauri and other wives of Nana.

Throughout the play it becomes evident that the female characters remain silent, without any voice or an expression of their views and feelings. The women presented in the play come from different socioeconomic strata. Gulabi, is a courtesan and Gauri is a poor Brahmin's daughter. But their fate is similar. Urbashi Bharat writes in "Gender and Power in Ghashiram Kotwal"

"As a courtesan Gulabi has no power over her own body, which she must exploit to attract the interest of man if she is to survive. Gauri has no power over hers either. The one person she can hope will protect her uses her instead to further his own interests, persuading himself, no doubt that by doing so he is only ensuring the success of hers. She does not express her feelings when she is handed over by her father to a man old enough to be her father to be used sexually for his own satisfaction and sense of power."

Guari compared to Gulabi lives even more dependently. She does not have financial independence that Gulabi has and she has to give up her purity, respectability for her survival and she lives even for short time as Nana throws her form his life when he has no further use of her.

Neela Bhalla writes in "**Ghashiram Kotwal Text and Sub-text**".

"The playwright had at least two choices in emphasizing Gauri's marginalized status. He could have given her a voice to protest and rage against being used as a commodity. The social structure of the period not permitting that he could have allowed readers to share her experiences of shame and humiliation. He does neither. Gauri's natural dreams of love and fulfillment are shattered at a very tender age, when she is called upon to become Nana's mistress.

She is discarded after being used and even her death is not accorded any importance. The reader learns about it through Ghashiram and it is his agony that we are witness to not Gauri's. Every last trace of her is wiped out. Nana wants no testimony of her life as of her death to be left behind. Her inner experience is rendered invisible. In fact the playwright even structurally marginalises her. Although on the one hand, the manner of the death underlines her insignificance, yet on the other the playwright's treatment of Gauri and her "Ostensible marginalisation" is ambiguous.

Can Tendulkar be seen along with dramatists like Albee, Ibsen and Shaw who "while being hailed as pioneers of the feminist cause were also critiqued for their male biases in their treatment of women? By confining Gauri mostly to stage directions and by structurally marginalizing her, the playwright has denied her the Brechtian self-awarness – the space between actor and character, which could have helped the actress playing Gauri's role to subversively use this space to undermine patriarchal notions of the role assigned to her by men. However this is not possible for Gauri. She has only one very short dialogue when she appears as shy and diffident a little awed by Nana's presence. Then she appears only in stage direction once during the Radha Krishna dance, where she is seductive and sensuous leading Nana on and second time during the Rangpanchami dance, young, vital and happy. In none of her three appearances, are there any hints of her reluctance or misery. One has to accept that Gauri's position is singular, as compared with the other women in Tendulkar's plays. She belongs to another era, Marriage of young girls to old and powerful rich men were nothing unusual as Nana's nine marriages testify. All the women protagonists of his other plays belong to post-independent India, women who could make free choice, In short, Tendulkar has examined the very contemporary issue of the relationship between power and gender in patriarchy in a historical setting with historically recognizable characters.

6. DRAMATIC TECHNIQUES IN GHASHIRAM KOTWAL

The play has a great theatrical importance in Indian Theatre. During the last two decades particularly, Indian theatre has gone back to indigenous, folk forms which are different from western theatrical expressions and yet relevant to our times. This urge for a fresh outlook in theatre has found wide expressions in many languages including Bengali Manipuri, Marathi Gujarati, Kannada, Malayalam and Hindi. A number of talented younger playwright. Directores, actors and designers have begun groping for a new vocabulary, for new styles and forms in their specific regions. It was in the 1960s and 70s that the urge to find a new and specifically Indian theatrical language acquired urgency. This urge has mainly been directed towards exploring the traditional and folk forms of our theatre or alternatively Sanskrit theatrical traditions with all its possibilities for imaginative productions.

Modern playwrights have written plays in which elements from one or more of the traditional forms have been used to create a new kind of dramatic structure. Tendulkar was the foremost dramatist who had changed the form and pattern of Indian drama by demolishing the three act play and creating exciting new models. By developing the flexible as well as carefully crafted forms, modes of recitation and storytelling specific to Maharastra he has managed to bridge the gulf between traditional and modern theatre by creating a vibrant new theatrical form an example of which is the play "Ghashiram Kotwal".

Tendulkar uses the Dashavatara a traditional Semi-classical form to investigate a contemporary political problem – the emergence of "demons" in public. The Dashavatar was performed in Konkan and Goa after harvesting. The folk-dance drama is based on the ten incarnations of Vishnu, namely, Matsya, Kurma, Varaha, Narsinha, Vaman, Parshuram, Ram, Krishna, Buddha and Kalki. The theme portrayed was the destruction of evil. The sutradhar informally introduced the drama. The speeches were extempore with the entry of the demons, Colour powder was thrown and there was much noise and jumping. Tendulkar uses mime and music of the Dashavatar plays in "Ghashiram Kotwal."

The play opens with Music as hymn to Ganapatiji is done by twelve man who sing the invocation song to Ganpati, the god of luck. He is later joined by Saraswatiji, Goddess of music and wisdom and Lakshmi, the goddess of wealth, such musical opening of the play reminds the tradition of classical Sanskrit drama and its aim is to arouse the interest of the audience to instill a feeling of seriousness and to arrest their attention.

The play belongs to the folk type Tamasha. The Tamasha of Maharashtra was born in the eighteenth Century out of Kirtinia (Kirtan), the oral tradition and different forms of music. It was performed by a roving troupe of about seven to eight actors, comprising of a dancer, a comedian a main actor and a chorus. The dancer performed the lavni, the comedian or the Songadya played with words and actions. The musical instrument was the 'dholki' and "tuntune" somewhat like dafli. Tamashas were popular during fairs and festivals and were great by patronised during the time of Sawai Madhav Rao Peshwa nd Baji Rao II. There are five divisions to The Thamasha.

1) The Gan stot,

An Invocation to Lord Ganesha

2) The Gaulan – the dance of Lord Krishna and "gopi's"

3) The lavni where the dance dances to the accompaniment of love songs which are suggestive.

4) The Vag – enactment in prose and verse of a story of adventure and romance.

5) And finally the Mujra where the dance is a close paralled to the "Saki" an influence that can be ascribed to the Moghul impact on local entertainment.

Tamasha has been kept alive by prominent dramatists like P. L. Deshpande Vasant Bapat and Vijay Tendulkar. In Ghashiram Kotwal Tendulkar uses many of these elements. He combines the ready wit of the Tamasha with the mime and music of the Dashavatar plays. The humour of the Songadya lay in his quick repartee and in his use of words with double entendre. This is a very integral part of Tendulkar's play. For example.

Sutradhar – wait now, Wait now.

Hold your horses. Must you go?

Brahman – Forces? Whose forces? Foreign? English."

With the help of such dialogues, the playwright manages to keep a very fast and crisp pace.

The central theatrical device in the play is the use of chorus. But as the play progresses they become the human curtain, alternately hiding the action and revealing bits of it as a peep show. In Marathi folk Drama, the role of the chorus was to serve the purpose of the refrain. But, here the scope of the chorus goes much beyond this. Besides the conventional role of repetition and commentary, the chorus participates in the action and selectively shields and reveals pictures of 18th century decadence and intrigue. It sometimes acts as a barrier and sometimes opens up like a door to provide glimpses of the action within. When the chorus turns its back on the audience we are to presume that the row of twelve Brahmins is no longer part of the action. Its participation is threefold. Some of the Brahmins from the human wall take on some specific minor individual roles. At such times they break off from the line. Secondly, they also become props like door, arches and temples. Their most significant participation is as vehicles of Satire, which works in two ways. They make direct satirical comments by slyly altering a word here and there in their refrain and also indirectly undermine the action on the stage.

The creation of the human curtain consisting of twelve Brahmins is an excellent dramatic device used by Tendulkar. As needed by the dramatist they may temporarily act as individuals but mostly function as a unit. At all important junctures in the play – the exposition, the installation of Ghashiram as Kotwal at Poona, at the time of his being stoned to death, and at the final carnival of three days – these twelve Brahmans are important witnesses to important events and also provide neutral comments. Their utterances are an integral part of the play and help the reader to clearly understand the intellectual and moral issues raised by the dramatist. This intermittent chanting of

"Shri Gajaraj Nartan Karen,

Hum to Poona ke Brahman Hain"

throughout the play establishes the play's link with folk drama.

As the play belongs to the folk type Tamasha which is basically musical but in which prose dialogues are also used to make social and political comment wherein the "Sutradhar" evolves as a significant dramatic tool as in the Sanskrit drama. The traditional function of the Sutradhar is to introduce the characters and initiate the events as well as comment on the action. Tendulkar makes a slight deviation in Ghashiram Kotwal by enhancing the role of the Sutradhar form that of a neutral observer and commentator to that of an active participant in the action of the play and an interlocutor who acts as a adhesive device bringing together the different and often disparate scenes of the play.

The Sutradhar plays the role of an interlocutor in the beginning as he stops a Brahman going furtively to Bavannakhani. There is much humour and discomfiture of the Brahman is evident. The sutradhar again stops three Brahmans – part of the human curtain – going to "the temple to hear religious discourses". The Sutradhar by asking incisive question cleverly pins them down into admitting their destination. The sutradhar continues to be a commentator throughout the play. When Ghashiram is thrown in jail, the sutradhar masquerades as a "fellow Prisoner". At other times, the Sutradhar teads the Chorus. Sutradhar : nine court Nana only thought of Gauri

All : Thought of nothing else, Gauri.

Again, it is through the Sutradhar's persistent probing that the Nana's wedding plans are revealed dramatically. An account of Ghashiram's final humiliation and punishment is provided by the Sutradhar's running commentary. And his final comments are dense with meaning. "And in the end came the end." The Sutradhar who thus adorns multiple roles is made accomplish multiple functions.

Tendulkar has used songs and dance effectively which set the backdrop of the decadence of the Peshwas of Poona of the 18th century. The aptly placed songs provide the necessary dramatic relief in between tense situations. Sometimes they serve to reinforce the tense atmosphere. The "lavni" or love song not only highlights the sensuous and passionate element but also provides a comment on corruption. The juxtaposition of the 'lavani' with the "abhanga" or religious hymn serves to bring out the contradiction in social values and norms.

Following the 'Tamasha' convention, abusive language is used here and there in the play. The dialogues are often filled with sarcasm. Folk theatre invites participation from the audience. In the play, the sutradhar and Ghashiram address the audience directly.

Indeed, the play is an innovative experiment that offers a new direction to modern Indian Theatre.

7. CONCLUSION

None can deny the fact that literature of every time and space springs from the cultural ethos of that time and space. The natural accordance is always to be found between the literature of a particular time, space and society of that time and space. Literature springs from culture and hence with all its aesthetics it proves to be a social and cultural document of that particular time and space. The bond between literature and culture is an everlasting phenomenon. The basic reason why this tuning is to be found between literature and the cultural ethos is the commitment of the writer. Writer experiences a greater commitment to his time and space and writes with a vision of reality as well as responsibility. His aim is to see and sees the prevailing norms of his culture in a real sense of the term and so he becomes a committed person, a committed writer. His status as a writer would be futile if there is no sense of responsibility or tone of commitment in his works. The first thing that can be concluded on the basis of the present research work on Vijay Tendulkar's plays is that he is a playwright with a conscious sense of commitment. A writer, who desires to be aesthetic in his approach of writing, should in no way give himself consent to connive at the prevailing realities of his time, culture and society. Tendulkar remains faithful not only in observing those realities but also in displaying them through his plays. He is a dramatist with commitment to his time and country. His plays are adorned with aesthetic value but he does not try to escape form his commitment. It can be justified more elaborately on the basis of his plays.

As a playwright he holds a mirror through his works before the society which is very much Indian and the society finds its own reflection in that mirror. Nothing of Society – good and evil, high and low, black and white – remains, unseen or unnoticed to him. His plays present before the spectators both the sides of life of an average Indian.

Tendulkar as a playwright reflects both the sides of Indian life – the bright side as well as the dark one. As Gouri Ramanarayan aptly observes "with his exposure to Marathi theatre form childhood and journalistic background Vijay Tendulkar turned contemporary socio-political situation into explosive drama". He has dwelt on the alienation of the modern individual, satirized contemporary politics, forcefully depicted social and individual tensions, portrayed with finesse the complexities of human character and vigorously exploited man-woman relationship in several of his works. Significantly the themes which have engaged his most frequent attention, have been the plight of woman in a maledominated urban middle class society, and the husband-wife relationship as obtained in metropolitan centers like Bombay and Delhi. Vijay Tendulkar portrays the contemporary society and the predicament of man in it with a special focus on the morbidity in his plays. His plays touch almost every aspect of human life in the modern world and share the disillusionment of the post- modern intellectuals. However, he seems to highlight three major issues: gender, power and violence.

A close study of Vijay Tendulkar's plays reveals that Tendulkar is not a teacher or preacher. He is not one of those dramatists who use their medium in the service of their favourite socio-political ideology. He is not out to propagate any particular philosophy of life. Some critics have pointed out leftist interpretation to the plays like Ghashiram Kotwal, Kamala and Sakharam Binder. It shows that his plays are open to diverse interpretations and cannot be tied down to a single line of thinking. So the question whether Tendulkar writes for life's sake or art's sake is pointless. All that we can say is that he seems to favour socialist humanism but it should also be remembered that his plays do not revolve in the orbit of that ideology either.

It is significant to note most of Tendulkar's plays are gyno-centric. He was essentially dealing with a world, which in the guise of the modern ideal of nuclear family rejected woman's independence as a citizen, enforced traditional Hindu-Brahmin norms of behavior, crushed her attempts of gaining freedom and exercised a rigid control on her sexuality and productivity.

In Silence! Sakharam Binder and the Vultures, Tendulkar deals with the unconventional theme of sex and violence, but a shift in his concerns is evident when he professes emphatically that man is constantly and violently seeking after positions of power and he would work on this "basic theme" hereafter. In fact, he became aware of moral values in the modern political system. His dramatic creation reflects his concern for common man who, caught in the matrix of opportunistic ethics of modern world, feels alienated. **Ghashiram Kotwal** shows how a common man hero, seeking, power, confronts the people who are already in power and undergoes an organic change. Though, it is based on historical legend, is not actually a historical play. Unlike other dramatists Tendulkar finds a parallel running between antiquity and modernity. **Ghashiram Kotwal** tells the story of a person who, confronted with a world of hypocrisy and inhumanity, learns to play a careerist falling in line with prevailing ethics and becomes a martyr. The play gains in metaphoric dimension as the central character's obsession with power results in the loss of his identity. Ghashiram is transformed from an ordinary person to a tyrannical executor. The play also demonstrates how a historical event cast in folk theatre could be used to depict the evils perpetrated by a lecherous ruler who not only shuts his eyes to but also indirectly aggravates the material and moral decadence that has set in the society around him and who creates an avenging monster just to cover up his amorous life.

The success or failure of any work of art depends upon its appeal – whether that appeal proves to be transitory or everlasting. A work of art with an everlasting appeal always remains eternal. It will not be out of the way or excessive exaggeration if the same thing is said about Tendulkar's plays. We do notice even today victims like Kamala, Benare, Sarita, Rama, Lalita Guari in Society. At the same time we notice even today males likes Arun, Sakharam, Ramakant and Umakant, Jaisingh Jadav, Ghashiram etc. as long as such characters are there in our society, the appeal of his plays would remain intact. His plays will never lose the quality of relevance with which they have been written.

BIBLIOGRAPHY

PRIMARY SOURCES

- **Tendulkar, Vijay** – *Collected Plays in Translation,* (Oxford University Press, 2003.)

- **Tendulkar, Vijay** – *Ghashiram Kotwal,* Seagull Books, Calcutta,   2002

SECONDARY SOURCES

- **Abrams M.H.** *"A Glossary of Literary Terms"* Macmillian. 1996

- **Abrams Teera**, *"Folk Theatre in Maharashtrian Social Development programme,"* Educational Theatre Journal 1975

- **Babu M.R.** *Political Deformity, In Indian drama Today,* Prestige - Books – 1990

- **Babu M.S.** *"Spiritual Deformity," In Indian Drama Today,* Prestige Books – 1990.

- **Babu, Sarat M.** *"Indian Drama Today",* New Delhi, Prestige Books, 1997

- **Banerjee Arundhati**, *Introduction Five plays by Vijay Tendulkar ,* Oxford up, Bombay

- **Bhalla M. M,** *"Folk Theatre and operas",* A Handful of Dreams Kantas Book Depot, 1977, Delhi.

- **Bhasin Kamala & Khan Nighat** Said *"Some questions on Feminism and its relevance in South Asia,"* ISBN New Delhi - 1993.

- **Bhatnagar M.K.** *"Indian writings in English"* Atlantic publishers, New Delhi.

- **Bhatnagar M.K.**, *Feminist English Literature,* Atlantic Publishers New Delhi

- **Bhave Pushpa** *"Vijay Tendulkar : A Study in Contemporary Indian Theatre"*, Sangit Natak Akademi, New Delhi – 1989.

- **Bhayani Utpal** – *સામાજિક નાટક, એક નૂતન ઉન્મેષ: વિજય તેડુંલકર,* NavBharat Sahitya Mandir 1993.

- **Das Bijay Kumar** – *Critical Essay on post-colonial literature,* Atlantic Publishers.- 2001

- **Das Bijay kumar.** *"Comparative Literature,"* Atlantic Publishers, New Delhi.

- **Deshpande G.P** *"Modern Indian Drama,"* An Anthology, Sahitya Akademi, New Delhi 2002

- **Dharan N.S.** *"The plays of Vijay Tendulkar"* Creative Books – New Delhi – 1999

- **Dharan N.S.** *"The Plays of Vijay Tendulkar",* Creative Books, 1999

- **Dhawan R.K.** *"20 years of Indian writing",* IAES, New Delhi 1999.

- **Dodiya J.K. & Surendran K.V.** *"Indian English Drama, Critical Perspectives,"* Sarup & Sons – 2002

- **Gargi, Balwant.** *Theatre in India,* New York: Theatre Arts, 1962.

- **Gayle Greene and Coppelia Kahn**, *"Feminist scholarship and the Social construction of woman,"* Making a Difference : Feminist Literary criticism, London, Methuen – 1985.

- **George, K.M., ed.** *Comparative Indian Literature,* Madras: Macmillan, 1984.

- **Gowda, Anniah.** *Indian Drama,* Mysore: Univ. of Mysore, 1974.

- વણકર ભી. ન – અનુસંધાન, ગુર્જર એજન્સી, ગાંધીમાર્ગ, અમદાવાદ.

- વણકર ભી.ન. – નવોન્મેષ, ભગવતી ઓફસેટ, અમદાવાદ

- વણકર ભી. ન. – દલિત સાહિત્ય, પૂનમ ઓફસેટ, ગાંધીનગર

- **Jyenger, K.R.S.,** *Indian writing in English,* Sterling publishers – 1985. New Delhi

- **Karnad Girish** *"Author's Introduction,"* Three Plays, Oxford University press, Delhi, 1994.

- **Karnad Girish** *"Nag Mandal"* & *"Hayavadana,"* Oup – 1993.

- **Kumar, Geeta** *"Portrayal of Women in Tendulkar's Shintata Court Chalu Ahe,"* New Directions in Indian Drama. New Delhi, Prestige – 1994.

- **M. Sarat Babu** *"Vijay Tendulkar's Ghashiram Kotwal,"* A Reader's Companion, Asia book Club – New Delhi – 2003.

- **Madge V.M.-** *Vijay Tendulkar's Plays: An Anthology of Recent Criticism,* Pencraft International, 2007

- **Mehta Jay** – *Zankhi: Glimpse of Marathi Drama and Literature,* Unique offset

- **Naik M.K.** *"A History of Indian English Literature,"* Sahitya Akademi, New Delhi – 1982

- **Naik M.K. and Mokashi S. Punekar,** *Perspectives on Indian Drama in English,* Oxford UP – 1977, Madras

- **Pandey S. and Freya Barwa** – *New Directions in Indian Drama* Prestige Books.

- **Reddy, Bayapa P**. *Studies in Indian writing English with a Focus on Indian English Drama,* New Delhi: Prestige, 1990.

- **Reddy, Venkata K**. *Critical Studies in Commonwealth Literature,* New Delhi: Prestige, 1994.

- **Sarat Babu M.** – *Vijay Tendulkar's Ghashiram Kotwal,* Asia Book Club, 2003

- **Sharma Vinod Bala** *"Critical Perspectives Ghashiram Kotwal"* Asia book club- 2001.

- **Sharma Vinod Bala** *"Critical Perspectives Ghasiram Kotwal",* Asia Book Club, 2001

- **Shiply Joseph J.** *Dictionary of World Literary Terms,* New Delhi: Doaba House, 1993.

- **Srinivas M.N. ,** *Social change in Modern India,* Orient Longman – 1972

- **Surendran K.V.** *"Indian Writing : Critical perspectives Sarup & Sons."* New Delhi

- **Taraporewala Freya and Pandey Sudhakar** *"Contemparary Indian Drama,"* New Delhi, Prestige Book - 1990

- **Tendulkar Vijay** *Katha* – 2001

- **Vatsyaya, Kapila**. *Traditional Indian Theatre:* Multiple Streams, New Delhi: National Book trust, 1980.

- **Veena Noble Dass** – *"Studies in Contemporary Indian Drama,"* Prestige – 1990.

ARTICLES FROM NEWSPAPERS

- **Rajadhyaksha Mukta**, Times of India – Monday, January 29, 2007., "Times review / Book Mark., "Vijay Tendulkar answers Some questions."

- **Times News Network** "Times of India" Tuesday, May 20, 2008.

- **The Hindu** 3/10/04., The Hindu - Sunday, September 16, 2001.

WEB SOURCES

http://www.rediff.com/news/2008/may/19vijay.htm (died article)

http://www.imdb.com/name/nm0854919/ (biography)

http://en.wikipedia.org/wiki/Vijay_Tendulkar (biography)

http://www.littleindia.com/news/123/ARTICLE/3138/2008-07-15.html (By:

Shekhar Hattangadi)

http://www.hinduonnet.com/thehindu/mag/2005/11/06/stories/2005110600310500.htm (**A rich

tapestry of women's stories**) Sunday, Nov 06, 2005 on kamala

http://salaamtheatre.org/kamala2004.html

www.urdutech.net/.../2008/05/vijaytendulkar.jpg

chat.indiatimes.com/articleshow/753698.cms

www.sajaforum.org/2008/05/obit-vijay-tend.html

http://news.bbc.co.uk/2/hi/south_asia/7407808.stm (death article)

www.hindu.com/.../stories/2007012002590800.htm (ghasiram) (Saturday, Jan 20, 2007)

http://www.hindu.com/mp/2007/01/20/images/2007012002590801.jpg

http://kpowerinfinity.spaces.live.com/Blog/cns!EEA9A8ECBFC1B50B!309.entry (((kanyadaan performance article) (August 11

Vijay Tendulkar's 'Kanyadaan' - An Unparalleled Performance)

www.indiaclub.com/shop/AuthorSelect.asp?Autho... (kanyadaan poster)

http://geekydood.wordpress.com/2008/04/30/silence-the-court-is-in-session/

http://www.quillandink.netfirms.com/Theatrecian/tcreview060506.htm (silence)

www.alibris.com/.../author/Tendulkar,%20Vijay (image)

http://timesofindia.indiatimes.com/articleshow/23796750.cms (article on ghasiram kotwal's performance) (30 Sep 2002, 2309)

http://picasaweb.google.com/suman.nsd/100MEDIA#5196466031138807074 (ghasiram kotwal)

http://www.mumbaitheatreguide.com/dramas/hindi/sakharam_binder_retold.asp (sakharam binder , performance article and photo)

http://www.sepiamutiny.com/sepia/archives/000636.html (photo sakharam binder)

http://www.iaac.us/Tendulkarfestival/VijayTendulkar.htm (photo with cast of sakharam binder)

http://www.bookrags.com/wiki/Shantata%21_Court_Chalu_Aahe (silence)

http://www.bookrags.com/wiki/Ghashiram_Kotwal

http://www.bookrags.com/wiki/Sakharam_Binder

http://www.bookrags.com/wiki/Vijay_Tendulkar

http://www.indianexpress.com/res/web/pIe/ie/daily/19991020/ile20071.html (article, Wednesday, October 20, 1999)

http://passionforcinema.com/a-conversation-with-sir-vijay-tendulkar/ (conversation with tendulkar)

http://shreevarma.homestead.com/bookreviews1.html

www.ingramcontent.com/pod-product-compliance
Lightning Source LLC
Chambersburg PA
CBHW071055280326
41928CB00050B/2521